THE ALCESTER BRANCH

by
STANLEY C. JENKINS AND ROGER CARPENTER

Great Alne station, looking west towards Alcester in the late 1930s. LENS OF SUTTON

WILD SWAN PUBLICATIONS LTD.

THE ALCESTER BRANCH

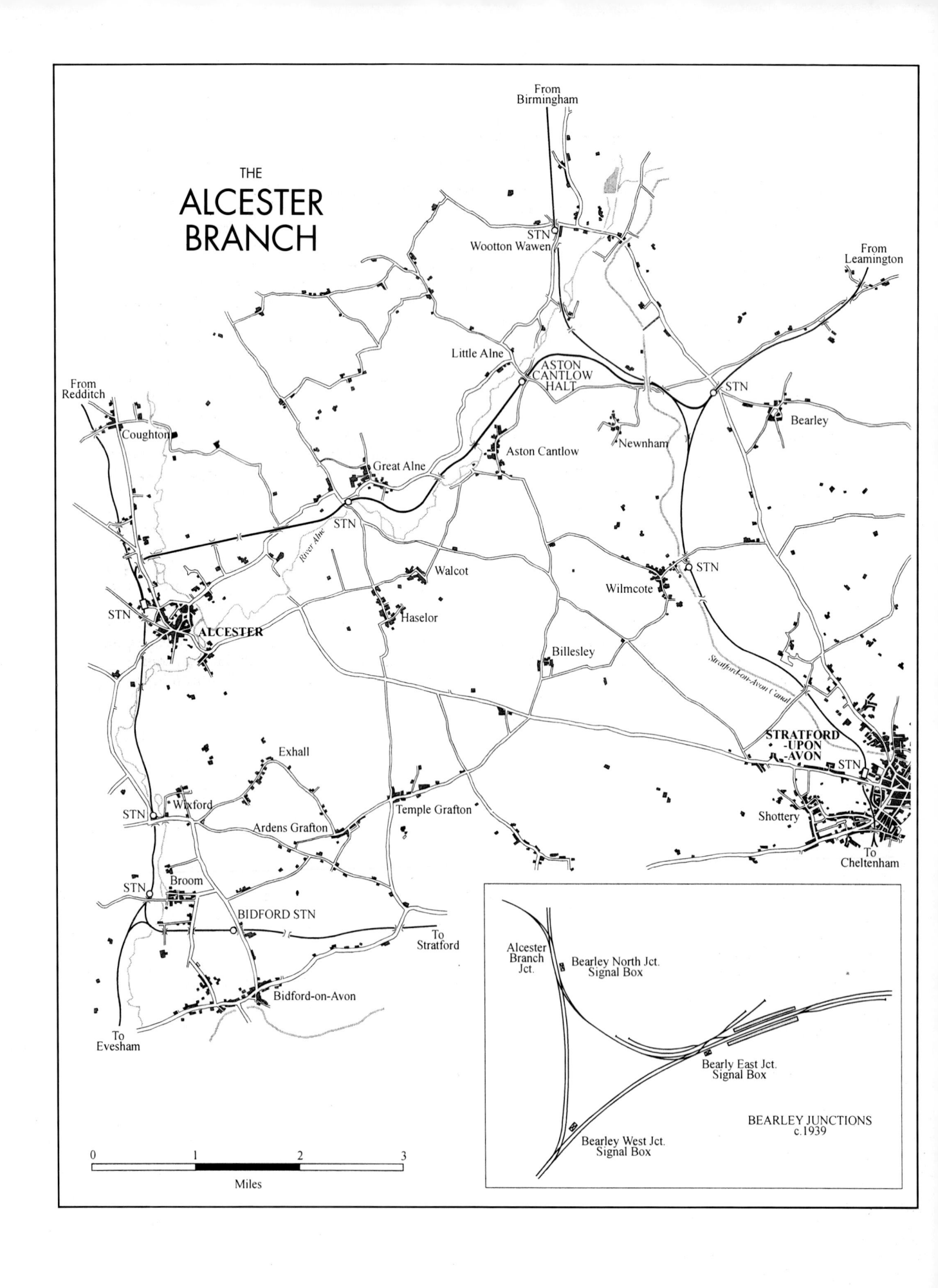

BEARLEY JUNCTIONS
c.1939

INTRODUCTION

Warwickshire is a neglected county as far as railway historians are concerned and apart from the considerable amount of attention that has been lavished on the Stratford-on-Avon & Midland Junction Railway, which crossed the county from east to west, there has been little published on the minor branch lines of this south Midlands region.

In railway terms the county was not without interest; it was served by four pre-Grouping companies including the SMJR (originally the East & West Junction Railway), the Midland Railway, the London & North Western Railway and the GWR. Most of the Great Western lines in Warwickshire were main lines, but there were also three branch lines – the Stratford-upon-Avon line, the short-lived Rowington to Henley-in-Arden branch and the Alcester branch; in addition, the North Warwickshire line functioned as a busy suburban route which also carried main-line traffic between the Midlands and the South West of England.

Of these rural Great Western lines, the six-mile single-track route from Bearley to Alcester was the one that most closely corresponds to our ideas of a 'classic' country branch line. It originated in the 1860s but had the misfortune to fall between the areas of two rival lines – the Midland and the GWR. This effectively prevented the route from being brought into existence until the following decade when the GWR and the Midland came to a somewhat uneasy arrangement whereby the branch would be built with Great Western help and worked as part of the GWR, while terminating in Alcester in a sort of 'joint' station shared by both companies, and with two station masters! Thereafter, the branch functioned as a typical GWR rural line until 1917, when it was closed as an emergency measure during World War One.

The Alcester branch was re-opened, with an additional stopping place at Aston Cantlow, in 1922–23, but its subsequent traffic receipts were disappointing, and the line was closed for a second time during World War Two. However, it was then re-opened again in 1941 to cater for workmen's traffic to and from Great Alne, where a factory had been hastily set up following wartime damage to Maudslay's engineering works in Coventry.

Following a further withdrawal of passenger services in 1944, the branch remained in use for wagon storage and occasional freight traffic until the 1950s, with final closure being effected in 1960.

The history of this little-known GWR line has never been the subject of a full monograph before, and it is therefore hoped that this present volume will fill a gap in the local history of a particularly attractive part of rural Warwickshire. The book is a collaborative venture between local railway enthusiast Roger Carpenter, who has spent many years assembling a large photographic archive of this, his favourite branch line, and Stanley C. Jenkins, a museum curator and social/transport historian.

Henley Street, Alcester, looking east from a postcard postmarked 'Alcester August 24th 1909'.

COLLECTION R. S. CARPENTER

CHAPTER ONE
ORIGINS OF THE ALCESTER BRANCH

ALCESTER, as its name implies, is a former Roman settlement on the River Alne, near the Roman Road known as Icknield Street. The area was conquered by the Anglo-Saxons after the Battle of Dyrham in 577 and, about fifty years later, the district became the home of a people known as the *Hwicce*; by the later Saxon period this area had been sub-divided into shires, one of which was Warwickshire while another was Worcestershire. Alcester was placed on the Warwickshire side of the boundary between these two counties, becoming the centre of a parish within the Hundred of Ferncumbe (later grouped with Pathlow to form the Hundred of Barlichway).

Alcester subsequently developed into a small, but relatively prosperous market town, with many picturesque timber-framed buildings and several local trades, including the manufacture of bricks and needles. The surrounding areas were predominantly agricultural, the only other towns in the immediate vicinity being Stratford-upon-Avon, which was some eight miles to the east, and Redditch, about the same distance away to the north.

The transport needs of the district were satisfied, at least in part, by the River Avon which flowed through Bidford, to the south of Alcester, and had been navigable up to Stratford-upon-Avon since 1639. Local traders were thus able to bring quantities of stone, coal or other materials into the area in craft up to 70ft long.

In addition to the River Avon, Icknield Street, the old Roman Road, gave Alcester residents a direct means of communication to and from Birmingham, though transport by coach or wagon remained very slow and expensive.

Water transport served for many years as the only viable means of moving heavy or cumbersome loads from one place to another. In this context it should be remembered that Britain is an island, and all of its historic centres of population were accessible by coastal or river craft. The development of industrial cities during the 18th Century, however, meant that for the first time major cities began to grow up away from the traditional arteries of river communication and were now connected by canals, most of which began life as extensions of existing natural waterways. The rapidly expanding industrial centre of Birmingham soon emerged as a nodal point in the new canal network, and it is still claimed (probably correctly) that this huge Midland city has 'more canals than Venice'.

In the 1790s it was decided that a canal link could be usefully provided between the Birmingham area and the River Avon at Stratford-upon-Avon, and in 1793 work began on the aptly-named Stratford-upon-Avon Canal between King's Norton Junction and Stratford.

The Stratford Canal was eventually completed throughout to Stratford-upon-Avon in 1816, and for the next few years the waterway functioned as part of a through route between Birmingham and the River Severn; in 1842 the Canal Company leased the Upper Avon between Stratford and Evesham, but any thoughts of further consolidation were rendered superfluous by the coming of rail transport – which made the existing canal system more or less obsolete.

EARLY RAILWAY DEVELOPMENT

Railway history in the Alcester and Stratford-upon-Avon areas can be traced back to the 1820s, when it was suggested that the Stratford Canal might be linked to the River Thames at Eynsham by means of a connecting tramway. This scheme, which would have been worked by horses, was somewhat ambitious for its time, but it nonetheless focused attention on the concept of longer-distance railways, and prepared the ground for more tangible schemes in the years to come. In the short term, it resulted in the opening of a 17-mile horse-worked line between Stratford and Moreton-in-Marsh on 5th September 1826.

In the following decade, it was proposed that a steam-worked railway could be built between Worcester and Oxford, and these tentative plans eventually found tangible form as the Oxford Worcester & Wolverhampton Railway.

The promoters of the Oxford Worcester & Wolverhampton line obtained their Act on 4th August 1845 (8 & 9 Vic. cap.184), and the OWWR was thereby empowered to begin construction of a main line commencing near Oxford by a junction with the GWR and terminating in the Grand Junction Railway station at Wolverhampton.

The OWWR scheme was, from its inception, seen as the Great Western's primary main line to the Midlands and the North, and for this reason it was planned as a double-track, broad-gauge route. Unfortunately, having led the OWWR promoters to believe that their expensive broad-gauge main line would be opened as a Great Western trunk route, the GWR then decided to adopt the Oxford & Rugby line as the principal broad-gauge main line to the Midlands, and in 1846 the Great Western obtained further powers for lines which would effectively carry the Oxford & Rugby route on to Wolverhampton in opposition to the OWWR.

The Oxford Worcester & Wolverhampton promoters felt – with complete justification – that the Great Western's action was a monstrous breach of faith, and the Oxford Worcester & Wolverhampton line was therefore constructed and opened as a 4ft 8½in gauge route, in open defiance of the GWR.

The OWWR line was opened between Stourbridge and Evesham on 1st May 1852, and on 4th June 1853 the route was opened for public traffic between Evesham and Wolvercot Junction, to the north of Oxford. Although, following pressure from the Great Western, this new main line was laid with mixed-gauge trackwork, it was worked entirely by standard-gauge locomotives and rolling stock as a more or less independent line (though GWR interests were still represented on the OWWR board).

In a desire to stimulate traffic in the largely rural areas through which their railway ran, the Oxford Worcester & Wolverhampton directors were keen to establish road feeder services which would connect their new railway with towns and villages that were not yet served directly by rail. Accordingly, in July 1853, it was reported that the OWWR company had made agreements with local carriers 'for the conveyance of passengers and goods from the OWWR to Witney, Winchcombe, Bridgnorth, Upton and Alcester'.

The OWWR thereby became the first railway to impinge upon Alcester and the surrounding villages, although the nearest railhead was still some eight miles away at Evesham.

Meanwhile, in a further development that could well have had important ramifications for the inhabitants of Alcester, the OWWR had taken the perhaps unusual step of purchasing the Stratford Canal. In addition, the Oxford Worcester & Wolverhampton company leased the horse-worked Stratford & Moreton tramway, which it then proceeded to work as a branch of its own system, with two horse-worked services each way daily.

It seems that the canal had been purchased for possible use as a railway that would run northwards to Birmingham. Such a line would clearly have been welcomed by the GWR which, at the time of the purchase, had not obtained Powers for the Birmingham & Oxford Junction route. When, however, the Great Western intimated that it would not require the trackbed of the canal for any future railways, the OWWR proceeded to operate the canal as a waterway.

Further developments took place at the end of the 1850s when the OWWR company constructed a 9½ mile single-track branch line from Honeybourne to Stratford-upon-Avon, which, opening to traffic on 12th July 1859, effectively replaced the northern end of the earlier Stratford & Moreton tramway.

In the interim, the Birmingham & Oxford Junction line had been opened on 1st October 1852 as a mixed-gauge extension of the existing Oxford & Rugby route, and when, on 14th November 1854, the Birmingham Wolverhampton & Dudley Railway was completed throughout to its junction with the OWWR route at Priestfield, the main-line railway system between Oxford and the Midlands was largely completed.

There were, in fact, two main lines between Oxford and Wolverhampton because, as we have seen, the Great Western directors had openly supported two, more or less parallel routes. In the short term this resulted in a major row between the GWR and OWWR companies, though in 1863 the OWWR (which had by then renamed itself the West Midland Railway) was amalgamated with the Great Western Railway.

DEVELOPMENTS AT STRATFORD-UPON-AVON AND ALCESTER

This main-line system, as brought into existence in the 1850s, formed part of a network of profitable lines, but it had omitted a number of smaller towns and regional centres, which were subsequently served by connecting branch lines.

The OWWR branch to Stratford-upon-Avon was soon joined by a further branch from Hatton, on the Birmingham & Oxford Junction line, to a temporary terminus in Birmingham Road, Stratford. This was opened by the nominally-independent Stratford-upon-Avon Railway on 10th October 1860, and worked by the GWR from the outset. The Stratford-upon-Avon Railway was laid to the mixed gauge, and it had intermediate stations at Claverdon, Bearley and Wilmcote.

On 1st January 1863 the former OWWR terminus at Sanctuary Lane in Stratford-upon-Avon (later known as Sanctus Street) was replaced by a new station in Alcester Road, and the Stratford-upon-Avon Railway from Hatton was then diverted into the new station.

These developments did much to satisfy the transport needs of farmers and traders in small towns and villages such as Stratford, Wilmcote and Bearley, but there was still considerable demand for improved rail links in the areas to the west of Stratford-upon-Avon.

In the meantime, the GWR was not the only railway to have shown an interest in the Warwickshire and Worcestershire areas – the rival Midland Railway was also well established, and this company was soon playing an important role in the creation of new branch-line schemes.

The Midland's interest can be traced back to the 1830s, when a company known as the Birmingham & Gloucester Railway was promoted with the intention of building a line running south-westwards from Birmingham. The Birmingham & Gloucester Railway was incorporated by an Act of 22nd April 1836, and its first section was opened, from Cheltenham to Bromsgrove, on 24th June 1840. The route was completed throughout to Birmingham, with running powers over the London & Birmingham Railway into Curzon Street station, on 17th December 1840. The Birmingham & Gloucester Railway was amalgamated with the Bristol & Gloucester to form the Bristol & Birmingham Railway in 1845, and in 1846 this new concern was itself absorbed by the Midland Railway Company.

The Midland was, from its inception, a powerful and ambitious company, and it was inevitable that, having acquired the Birmingham to Bristol main line, the MR should have embarked on a programme of expansion in the area. On 23rd July, 1858, for example, the Redditch Railway was incorporated with powers to build a 4½ mile branch from the former Birmingham & Gloucester main line at Barnt Green to Redditch. This short feeder line was opened to passenger traffic on 19th September 1859, and for freight traffic on 1st October 1859. All services were worked by the Midland Railway.

THE EVESHAM & REDDITCH RAILWAY
Further to the south, the Midland Railway was authorised to build a branch from its Bristol main line at Ashchurch to Evesham on 7th June 1861, and this line was opened to traffic on 1st October 1864. Finally, in connection with these schemes, the Evesham & Redditch Railway was promoted by local business interests, and on 13th July 1863 they managed to obtain an Act (26 & 27 Vic. cap.114) for the construction of a railway commencing at Evesham by a junction with the West Midland Railway and terminating in Redditch in connection with the Redditch Railway.

The Evesham & Redditch Railway had an authorised capital of £149,000, and the scheme was fully supported by the Midland Railway. Three years were allowed for the purchase of land, with a period of five years for completion of the works.

The new line was opened for freight traffic between Evesham and Alcester on 16th June 1866, and for passengers on 17th September 1866. The northern section of the line from Alcester to Redditch was completed on 4th May 1868, from which date the original terminus at Redditch was closed and all trains used the new station.

The Evesham & Redditch Railway was single track throughout, with stations at Harvington, Salford Priors, Wixford, Alcester, Coughton and Studley & Astwood Bank. (An additional stopping place was opened at Broom in 1879.) The line was worked by the Midland Railway as part of a circuitous, cross-country route between Barnt Green, Redditch, Evesham and Ashchurch.

THE WARWICK JUNCTION RAILWAY
The successful promotion of the Evesham & Redditch Railway was a source of obvious encouragement for local landowners and entrepreneurs, who were led to believe that companies such as the Midland Railway would assist them in the promotion of further lines; in this way it was hoped that rail communication could be extended to smaller towns and villages that had not, hitherto, enjoyed the advantages of the new form of communication.

With these thoughts in mind, group of local traders and landowners suggested that a short connecting line might be constructed between the existing Stratford-upon-Avon Railway at Bearley and the authorised route of the Evesham & Redditch Railway at Alcester. Such a line would bring cheap and efficient communication to people living in the parishes of Arrow, Kinwarton, Oversley, Haselor, Great Alne, Aston Cantlow, Bearley and Wootton Wawen, while at the same time opening up a useful direct line between Alcester, Stratford-upon-Avon and Warwick.

A company known as the Warwick Junction Railway was promoted locally with the aim of building the proposed line, but at this juncture problems arose when the Midland Railway refused to support the projected scheme. There was similar opposition from the Great Western Railway, the implication being that both companies viewed the suggested line as an unnecessary and expensive addition to a system that was now quite adequate for the needs of a rural area.

There was, on top of this, a very good reason why the Midland Railway and the GWR should have both refused to support the Warwick Junction line – these two companies had recently concluded an agreement under which they agreed to co-operate on all matters of dispute that might arise between the two railways. This agreement was designed to eradicate the kind of wasteful competition that had hitherto characterised relations between the rival companies, and it follows that if the Great Western did not want the Warwick Junction line to be built the Midland Railway would not have supported the scheme because such a move would have been against the spirit of the GWR-MR agreement.

There remained a possibility that the local promoters could still have proceeded with their scheme as an independent venture, but in reality there was little incentive for such schemes to proceed unless they were assured of at least some support from one or other of the main-line companies. Moreover, the failure of the banking firm of Overend, Gurney & Company in May 1866 led immediately to a huge financial crisis, and in these circumstances it became increasingly difficult for small, locally-promoted companies to raise their capital.

THE ORIGINS OF THE ALCESTER RAILWAY COMPANY
Despite these problems, the supporters of the hoped-for Alcester to Bearley line did not give up all hope of bringing their scheme to fruition, and in the early 1870s the project was revived by a group of landowners and entrepreneurs. The underlying financial situation had, by that time, considerably improved, whilst the connecting main-line companies were now less openly hostile.

It is difficult to identify the prime supporters of the revised scheme, though in retrospect it seems likely that the Alcester Railway evolved from the earlier Warwick Junction scheme, which had been promoted by Alcester traders and residents. There was a perceived need for some form of rail outlet to the east which would enable Alcester people to reach Warwick and Leamington Spa, as well as Stratford-upon-Avon. There is also a body of evidence to suggest that some of the supporters of the Stratford-upon-Avon Railway (which was still independent of the GWR) were by no means opposed to the idea of their line being extended westwards, and on this basis it is likely that informal links were established between the Alcester promoters and some of the Stratford-upon-Avon proprietors.

At the same time, the supporters of the Alcester Railway scheme were quietly lobbying the GWR and influential landowners, and by 1871 a body of support had been carefully built up in Alcester and the surrounding district. With everything now proceeding according to plan, the local newspapers began to take an interest in the scheme, and on Saturday 23rd March 1872 *The Redditch Indicator* informed its readers that:

> 'The Alcester Railway is to come from Bearley... A petition, signed by five Justices of the Peace, seventy manufacturers of Redditch and district, and by the leading tradesmen, will be presented to Parliament in favour of it. By this line, Redditch will be within seventeen miles of the Hatton station on the Great Western Line. The only opposition is that of the Midland Railway.'

Before putting their scheme into effect, the supporters of the Alcester Railway had to obtain an Act of Parliament, which would incorporate the company and enable it to purchase the necessary land by compulsory purchase if necessary.

Plans and sections of the proposed undertaking were deposited with a Clerk of the Peace for the County of Warwick on 30th November 1871, and in an atmosphere of renewed optimism, the promoters gave notice that they intended to present a Bill before Parliament in the coming session for the incorporation of the Alcester Railway Company, with powers for the construction and maintenance of a railway commencing in Bearley and terminating in Alcester.

The scheme was well supported by the tradesmen and manufacturers of the surrounding district, and, with further support and encouragement from the Great Western Railway and the Stratford-upon-Avon Railway, the Bill appeared to have every chance of success. The one discordant note was the attitude of the Midland Railway – though on this occasion the Midland's opposition was perhaps more symbolic than real; the MR was obviously concerned about the future arrangements at Alcester, but the Midland Railway Company appeared to have no particular objection to the line itself, and it was envisaged that Midland concerns would be addressed at the Committee stages as the Alcester Railway Bill passed through Parliament.

The Bill had a comparatively easy passage through the complex Parliamentary process, and having passed successfully through all stages, the Bill for 'Making a Railway in the County of Warwick from the Bearley Station of the Stratford-upon-Avon Railway to the Alcester Station of the Evesham & Redditch Railway' received the Royal Assent on 6th August 1872.

SOME DETAILS OF THE ALCESTER RAILWAY ACT

The resulting Act (35 & 36 Vic. cap.170) provided consent for the construction and maintenance of a railway 'with all proper stations, approaches, works and conveniences connected therewith' which would start at Bearley and terminate at Alcester. With meticulous accuracy, the route was defined as:

> 'A railway six miles three furlongs and five and a half chains in length, commencing by a junction with the Stratford-upon-Avon Railway at or near a point thereon one hundred and forty yards or thereabouts to the southward of the south-west corner of the new signal box of the Bearley Station on that railway, and terminating by a junction with the Evesham and Redditch Railway at a point thereon four hundred and sixty-two yards or thereabouts northward of the northern end of the passenger platforms of the Alcester Station on that railway.'

Capital of £50,000 in five thousand ten-pound shares was authorised, together with borrowing powers for a further £16,650 in loans. The minimum qualification for directorship was set at £150, and the number of directors would be five.

William Bevington Lowe, John William Kershaw, George Wyman, John Williams and William Jephcott were mentioned by name as the first directors of the Alcester Railway, and these gentlemen were to remain in office until the first ordinary meeting of the company. At that meeting the shareholders present in person or by proxy would be able to elect a new body of directors, or allow the original directors to continue in office.

A period of three years was allowed for the compulsory purchase of land, while five years were allowed for completion of the works.

Further provisions empowered the Alcester Railway to enter into agreements with the Great Western Railway and the Stratford-upon-Avon Railway for the operation and management of the railway, and the Stratford-upon-Avon Railway was allowed to subscribe up to half of the Alcester Railway's authorised capital.

Another clause dealt with the sensitive issue of running powers over the Evesham & Redditch Railway between the junction with the authorised route of the Alcester Railway and Alcester station. The Alcester Railway Company and all persons lawfully using that railway were allowed to run over the Evesham & Redditch Railway 'with their engines, carriages, wagons and trucks' between the point of junction and Alcester station in return for the payment of tolls and charges to be agreed between the companies concerned; in the event of a dispute, the matter was to be referred to the Board of Trade for arbitration.

As usual in those days, the Act contained elaborate provisions with respect to the various categories of traffic that might be carried on the Alcester Railway, the charges for each type of traffic being clearly set out. 'All coals, cinders, dung, compost, and all sorts of manure, lime and limestone, and all undressed materials for the repair of public roads', for example, would be charged at a rate not exceeding one penny halfpenny per ton per mile, but if conveyed in carriages belonging to the company an additional sum per ton per mile 'not exceeding one halfpenny' would be charged. If these carriages were propelled by an engine belonging to the company, an additional charge 'not exceeding one penny per mile' would be made, subject, however, to a maximum charge of one penny halfpenny per mile.

As far as passengers were concerned, the Act stated that the maximum rate of charge to be made by the company 'including the tolls for the use of the railway, and for carriages and locomotive power, and every expense incidental to such conveyance' would be no more than three pence per mile for first-class travellers, two pence per mile for second-class passengers and one penny halfpenny per mile for third-class bookings.

Each traveller would be allowed to take ordinary luggage 'not exceeding one hundred and twenty pounds in weight for first class passengers, one hundred pounds in weight for second class passengers and sixty pounds in weight for third class passengers' without any extra charges being made.

These provisions were little more than legal formalities, and it should be pointed out that identical or near-identical provisions were inserted into many other branch-line Acts during the 19th century. Nevertheless, the proposed carriage tolls provide an interesting glimpse into the various types of traffic that were expected to flow over a country branch line at that time, and for this reason some of the provisions have been summarised in *Table 1* (below).

TABLE 1
Proposed Scale of Charges on the Alcester Railway Act 1872

Type of Traffic	Basic Rate per mile	Use of Vehicle	Maximum Charge
Coal, cinders, dung, compost, manure, limestone, etc (per ton)	1½d.	½d.	1½d.
Sugar, grain, corn, flour, hides, timber, nails, anvils, chains, etc (per ton)	3d.	1d.	3d.
Cotton, wools, drugs, manufactured goods, merchandise, fish, etc (per ton)	3½d.	1d.	4d.
Carriages and other road vehicles (per mile)	6d.	2d.	6d.
Horses and beasts of burden	3d.	1d.	4d.
Cows, bulls and other cattle	3d.	1d.	3d.
Calves, pigs, sheep, etc	1d.	¼d.	1d.
First Class Passengers	2d.	1½d.	3d.
Second Class Passengers	2d.	1½d.	2d.
Third Class Passengers	2d.	1½d.	1½d.
Boilers, cylinders or other items of great weight up to 8 tons (per mile)	n/a	n/a	1s.
Items exceeding 8 tons	n/a	n/a	Such sum as they 'think fit'

AN AGREEMENT WITH THE GREAT WESTERN RAILWAY

The promoters had not been idle while their Bill was before Parliament, and in July 1872 a group of Alcester Railway supporters, including William Lowe, George Wyman and John Kirshaw had signed a tripartite agreement whereby the Alcester Railway would be worked by the GWR in connection with the Stratford-upon-Avon Railway at Bearley.

It was agreed that the Alcester Railway Company would pay the GWR fifty per cent of the operating receipts, and that there would be no rent or other charges for the use of the facilities at Bearley station until such time as the Alcester Railway was able to pay dividends of 5 per cent per annum. Any rents or other charges which might then be paid for the use of the junction station would be decided by agreement.

All staff needed to operate the railway after its opening would be provided and employed by the GWR, and the latter company would also supply all 'locomotive power, engines, carriages, trucks, rolling stock, plant, stores material and labour' that would be needed for the proper and sufficient working of the railway – the only officer to be provided by the Alcester company being the Secretary.

In addition to arranging this formal working agreement, it seems that the GWR was already helping the Alcester Railway in a number of other ways, most importantly by suggesting that the local company should engage William Clarke as Engineer. This little-known consulting engineer appears to have been one of the Great Western's regular consultants, and while not actually employed by the GWR, he obviously enjoyed a close association with the GW company.

William Clarke, who had earlier worked in India on the Punjab Railway, was back in England by the 1860s, and he was then involved with a number of railways in the Shropshire and Welsh border areas, notably the Shrewsbury & Hereford Railway. By the 1870s, he was working for various smaller companies, most of these being locally-promoted lines which had turned to the Great Western for assistance; in today's parlance, this self-employed consulting engineer would perhaps be called a Great Western 'project manager', and he certainly filled this role in the case of the Alcester Railway, being responsible for the initial surveys of the line, and other professional matters relating to the Parliamentary Bill from 1871 onwards.

Having obtained their Act of Incorporation, the supporters of the Alcester Railway were able to organise themselves into a properly-constituted Board of Directors, and on 6th November 1872 a small group of promoters met at Alcester to agree these formalities.

The meeting was attended by George Wyman, William Jephcott, John Williams, John Jones (the Company Solicitor) and John Coulson Bull – three of these individuals being provisional directors of the company. It was agreed that Mr Wyman would take the chair for the purposes of the meeting, while John C. Bull was formally appointed as Secretary to the company. It was decided that the offices of the Alcester Railway would be in John Bull's offices in Warwick, and the promoters then turned their attention to the working agreement that had recently been arranged with the GWR. It was resolved that the seal of the Alcester Railway Company should be affixed to the agreement, leaving the date of the agreement as 12th July 1872 (in other words the directors decided that the operating agreement could be signed retrospectively!).

There was, thereafter, little more that could be done until sufficient capital had been subscribed, though in the next few weeks there was evidently considerable contact between the local company and the GWR. There was also a subsequent change in the composition of the Alcester Railway Board of Directors, in that George Wyman, William Jephcott and John Williams were replaced by the Earl of Yarmouth and Sir Charles Alexander Wood – who later became the Chairman and Deputy-Chairman respectively – while William Lowe and John Kirshaw continued to serve as ordinary directors.

The appearance of Sir Charles Alexander Wood was highly significant in that he was the then Deputy-Chairman of the Great Western Railway, and his presence on the Alcester Railway board underlined the GWR's commitment to the new scheme. Similarly, William B. Lowe and John W. Kirshaw both represented the Stratford-upon-Avon Railway, Mr Lowe being its Chairman, and, although both men were Warwickshire residents, their roles as directors of the Alcester Railway probably had much to do with the £25,000 that was being subscribed to the scheme by the Stratford-upon-Avon company.

On 13th February 1873, William Lowe, Sir Charles Alexander Wood, John Kirshaw, the Earl of Yarmouth, and John Bull (the Company Secretary) attended a meeting at Paddington at which it was reported that 314 shares had been allotted and the whole of the calls on them had been paid. The Secretary reported that he had deposited a copy of the Alcester Railway Act of Parliament with the Clerk of the Peace for the County of Warwick, and it was then agreed that William Clarke would proceed with a survey of the line so that plans of the land required could be drawn up.

The agreement with William Clarke under which he had prepared the initial plans and assisted with the application to Parliament was referred to Charles Alexander Wood and Sir Daniel Gooch, and the Secretary was requested to 'wait upon the landowners with a view to the purchase of the land' as soon as the necessary plans were ready.

A 'POLITICAL' LINE?

On a footnote, it may seem strange that the Great Western Railway should have shown such an active interest in the Alcester Railway scheme of 1872 when, just six years before, the company had exhibited no interest in the abortive Warwick Junction proposal.

In practice, the GWR was clearly aware of various other schemes which were then being discussed in relation to the extension of existing minor lines across the South Midlands towards the South Wales coal fields. One of these lines was the grandly-titled 'Midland Counties & South Wales Railway', which had earlier obtained powers for a line from Blockley to Ross-on-Wye, with running powers over the Ross & Monmouth Railway and over the Midland Railway between Bickford and Tewkesbury.

Although the Midland Counties & South Wales scheme had been badly hit by the 1866 financial crisis, it was showing signs of revival by the early 1870s, while another company, known as the East & West Junction Railway, was also active in the area to the east of Stratford-upon-Avon. The complex history of these impoverished, but highly ambitious companies is too complex to go into here, though it is worth mentioning that in 1873 the Evesham Redditch & Stratford-upon-Avon Railway was empowered to construct a railway commencing by a junction with the Stratford-upon-Avon station of the East & West Junction Railway and terminating at Broom in connection with the Evesham & Redditch Railway.

The proposed Stratford & Broom Junction line was only about six miles to the south of the Alcester Railway and, in view of the obvious threat to Great Western interests in this area, it clearly made sense for the GWR to support the Alcester Railway as a counter-move; to that extent it seems likely that the Great Western's interest in the Alcester route owed more to the shifting sands of railway politics than to any purely economic considerations. Nevertheless, for whatever reason, GWR support was now guaranteed, and in the early part of 1873 the supporters of the Alcester Railway could look forward to a successful accomplishment of their scheme.

CHAPTER TWO

CONSTRUCTION AND OPENING OF THE BRANCH

IN engineering terms the route of the proposed Alcester Railway from Bearley to Alcester presented few problems. Commencing by its junction with the Stratford-upon-Avon Railway, the authorised route ran north-westwards for a little under two miles and then curved south-westwards into the valley of the River Alne. The river was followed for about four miles, after which the route diverged westwards, away from the river, and across an intervening spur of slightly higher land; beyond, the authorised line descended towards its junction with the existing line of the Evesham & Redditch Railway some 20 chains to the north of Redditch station.

There would be no tunnels or major earthworks, though relatively small cuttings were required at the miniature 'summit' near Alcester and at other places along the 6 mile 35½ chain route. It was estimated that some 186,878 cubic yards of material would have to be excavated from the cuttings, all of this material being soft earth.

The low-lying nature of the riverside meadows through which the line would run for much of its length meant that several lengthy stretches of embankment would be needed, and these, in turn, would be pierced by a number of under-line drains and culverts. There would also be two small viaducts across the rivers Alne and Arrow. It was calculated that the embankments would consume approximately 125,179 cubic yards of material, all of this being obtained as spoil from the cuttings.

As originally planned, the line would have been spanned by five public or private road overbridges, but in the event this number was eventually reduced to four by the elimination of one of the roads concerned; there were two road underbridges, both of which would span public roads.

The principal landowners included the Earl of Abergavenny, who owned much of the land required for the railway in the parish of Aston Cantlow, the Marquis of Hertford, whose land holdings were concentrated at the western end of the route, and various members of the Hemming family who owned and occupied a large amount of the agricultural land required for the new line in and around Great Alne.

John Hemming Senior and Amy Hemming appear to have been the main owners or occupiers of the land in the parish of Great Alne, but the Book of Reference prepared in connection with the 1872 Parliamentary Bill shows that other members of the same family, including John Hemming Junior and Joseph Hemming, were also involved.

An estimate of expenses had been prepared by William Clarke in December 1871, and on this basis the company's authorised capital of £50,000 had been determined. The estimate itself is of some interest in that it provides useful details of the work that would be required, and the main items of expenditure are set out in *Table 2*.

TABLE 2
William Clarke's Estimate of Expenses for Construction of the Line

Item	£	s.	d.
186,878 cubic yards of earthworks at 10d. per yard	7,786	11	8
125,179 cubic yards of embankments	521	11	7
Public road bridges (total six)	4,300	0	0
Accommodation bridges and works	2,240	0	0
River bridges, drains and underline culverts	2,408	0	0
Metalling of roads and level crossings	80	0	0
Gatekeepers' lodges	170	0	0
6 miles 35½ chains of permanent way (single line)	14,820	12	6
Permanent way for sidings and cost of junctions	1,400	0	0
Stations	4,000	0	0
Contingencies (ten per cent)	3,772	13	6
Land and buildings	8,400	0	0
TOTAL COSTS	£49,899	9	3d.

Tenders for the construction of the line were received in the Spring of 1873, and on 29th May 1873 the directors were informed that no less than thirteen tenders had been sent in. These ranged from £53,297 16s. 6d. to as little at £26,211 16s., the highest tender being that received from Joseph Chapel, while the lowest was submitted by Thomas Witham Chester. On William Clarke's advice the directors awarded the contract for construction of the line to Messrs Scott & Edwards of Melmerby, Yorkshire; their estimate of £31,801 10s. 1d. corresponded quite closely to the Engineer's own estimate of £30,758 1s. 7d.

CONSTRUCTION BEGINS

The work of building the line was probably under way by the summer of 1874, although the directors' minutes provide little information regarding the progress of the works. The line would certainly have been staked out throughout its length by the summer of 1874, and the major part of the earthworks and excavation was probably completed by the first months of 1875.

Not everyone was in favour of the railway. It seems that the wife of a local vicar objected to the railway on what today might be called 'conservation grounds', and in order to impede the work of railway builders she would go out late at night to remove the surveyor's stakes that had been placed along the route. These minor acts of sabotage were eventually discovered, and the navvies were then allowed to carry out their work in peace!

In March 1875 Messrs Scott & Edwards took delivery at Stratford-upon-Avon of a brand new Manning Wardle saddle tank locomotive for use on construction trains, and this suggests that the line was substantially completed by that time. The locomotive concerned was a standard 0–6–0ST (Works No. 517) with 3ft wheels and 13in × 18in inside cylinders. The engine, known as *Stanley*, was a classic

Great Alne around the turn of the century with the quiet pace of country life much in evidence. This photograph was taken on the Wootton-Wawen to Alcester road, facing Alcester close to the junction with Mill Lane. The mixture of timber-framed and red-brick buildings are typical of villages in this part of Warwickshire.
WARWICKSHIRE RECORD OFFICE (PH 352/4/25)

Manning Wardle industrial locomotive, with a square saddle tank and a simple 'bent sheet' cab; its coupled wheelbase was 5ft 10in + 5ft 8in, and its maximum height was 11ft 7in to the top of the chimney. (In the 1880s the engine was used on the construction of the Bembridge branch, in the Isle of Wight, and it was later purchased by the Isle of Wight Railway; in 1917 the locomotive was sent to Mesopotamia on war service.)

With the new railway taking shape in the pleasant Warwickshire countryside, the directors turned their attention to the matter of intermediate stations. In June 1874 a memorial had been received from the inhabitants of Aston Cantlow, who asked if a station could be provided to serve their needs. There were also plans for a small station at Great Alne, and in this context James Grierson, the GWR General Manager, was sent to the district in order that a decision could be made on the basis of his advice.

On 23rd June 1874 the General Manager reported that he had visited the locality, and he recommended that, as a man would have to be stationed at Great Alne to work the level crossing which would be needed at that place, one of the stations should be built there. He suggested that the new station should be as small as possible as the potential traffic was unlikely to be very significant. He also suggested that a similar station might be erected at Aston Cantlow, but the site of this stopping place would be determined at a later date.

The new station at Great Alne was said to be 'almost complete' by the summer of 1875, while the additional facilities that would be needed at Bearley had been commenced by that date. Little progress had been made at the other end of the line as there had been no agreement with the Midland Railway vis-à-vis the facilities that would be necessary. Despite this minor problem, most of the line was more or less complete by the Autumn of 1875.

In August 1875 it was reported that the earthworks had been formed throughout from Bearley to Alcester, and the whole of the masonry work in the bridges and culverts was complete. The station works were in a forward state and nearly the whole of the permanent way had been laid; work was progressing with the ballasting, although there had been some labour problems during the harvest period as many of the labourers engaged on the works had temporarily deserted the railway during the months of August and September. It was reported that total expenditure to 30th June 1875 had amounted to £49,667.

The line from Bearley to the point of junction with the Midland Railway at Alcester was finished by the early part of 1876, and on 14th February 1876 William Clarke reported as follows to the Alcester Railway directors:

The sleepy village of Aston Cantlow seen around 1900 was typical of the small farming communities in this part of Warwickshire, in which the way of life changed little over the 19th and early 20th centuries. Many of the buildings of timber frame and red brick construction with tile and later slate roofs dated from the 17th and 18th centuries – some even older. They contrasted sharply with the Victorian slums and industrial factories and waste lands that made up the areas of Birmingham and the Black Country a mere 25-30 miles to the north. AUTHORS' COLLECTION

Another idyllic scene showing Church Lane from around 1910, again showing small cottages of red brick and timber frame construction. Notice how the cottage in the background had been re-roofed in corrugated iron sheeting, a material that was just becoming available to local village communities at this period. Other modifications include the extensive use of 'brick nogging' – a form of construction in which some or all of the panels between the timbers are filled, not with wattle and daub, but with brickwork. AUTHORS' COLLECTION

'My Lords and Gentlemen,
The whole of the works of the railway between Bearley and the junction with the Evesham & Redditch Railway at Alcester have been completed, and are now ready for the Government Inspector.

'The new station building at Bearley, and the alterations and additions to the main line and the sidings there have, with the exception of some unimportant details, been carried out.

'The proposed works to be done in the station and junctions at Alcester have been approved by the Midland Company with whom, and with the Evesham & Redditch Railway, an agreement is now pending for the use of the station, and directly such is determined the junction and other needful works can at once be proceeded with.'

A few days later, on Saturday 19th February 1876, *The Redditch Indicator* recorded that work on the Alcester Railway was virtually complete, but the junction with the Evesham & Redditch Railway at Alcester 'had still to be made'. The paper added that it would 'be best for all concerned' if Alcester Railway trains were able to use the existing Alcester station, rather than a separate station as 'originally proposed'.

THE PROBLEMS AT ALCESTER

In fact, the difficulties experienced in coming to an amicable agreement with the Midland Railway in respect of the station and junction facilities at Alcester had been greater than anticipated and, as mentioned by *The Redditch Indicator*, the Alcester Railway had, at one stage, threatened to proceed with the construction of a separate terminal station alongside the Midland Railway establishment!

As originally planned, the Alcester Railway would have converged with the MR at Alcester Junction and continued southwards alongside it for a short distance before terminating in the Evesham & Redditch station. The layout of the existing station would probably have precluded the installation of a bay platform for Alcester Railway trains, and no bays were shown on the original plans prepared by William Clarke in connection with his first surveys of the projected line in 1871.

It is also unclear if the existing Evesham & Redditch line would have been used by Alcester Railway trains, or if a separate 'third line' would have been constructed alongside the up and down MR running lines. On the other hand, the published plans show that terminal facilities would have been provided beside the Midland Railway goods yard – a double-track engine shed and locomotive turntable being tentatively shown immediately to the north of the Midland goods shed.

None of these options presented any technical problems and, as the Evesham & Redditch Railway was itself no more than a rural branch line carrying limited traffic, there is no doubt that Alcester Railway trains could easily have been accommodated in the existing station without causing undue congestion.

The real problem stemmed from inability of the Midland Railway to agree that the Evesham & Redditch station could be used by Great Western trains on terms and conditions that were acceptable to all parties. The Alcester Railway at first suggested that the Evesham & Redditch station might be used at an annual rent of £150, with additional contributions to the station's working expenses in proportion to the traffic carried by each company.

The Midland Railway seemed reasonably happy with the proposed rental and contribution to working expenses, but it proved far more difficult to reach agreement in respect of the cost of extra facilities that would be needed at Alcester in connection with the new line from Bearley.

The facilities in question would be the actual junction itself, together with at least one additional running line between the junction and the existing crossing loop, and various extra terminal facilities including a locomotive shed and turntable. These arrangements would also involve alterations and additions to the existing signalling system at the Evesham & Redditch station.

All of these new works were to be provided on land belonging to the Evesham & Redditch Railway and, as such, it was necessary for William Clarke, on behalf of the Alcester Railway, to reach agreement with both the Evesham & Redditch Railway and the Midland company.

In a memorandum dated 4th August 1875 William Clarke reported that his estimates for the cost of the necessary alterations at Alcester were £504 10s. less than the estimates that had been provided by the Midland Railway. On this basis the Directors of the Alcester Railway intimated that they would perhaps be better off if they constructed their own station next door to the existing station – although it was recognised that this course of action would not be in the best interests of the travelling public.

AN AGREEMENT WITH THE MIDLAND RAILWAY

The threat to build a separate station was probably no more than a bluff, though sufficient land for such a station was available. In the end, it was agreed that the Midland Railway would construct the new facilities and carry out the necessary alterations to the track and signalling at Alcester. The cost of the new works would be paid for by the Alcester Railway and the Evesham & Redditch Railway as part of a complicated financial arrangement whereby the Alcester company would pay interest and rent to the Evesham & Redditch company, while the Evesham company would itself make payments to the Alcester Railway so that the latter company could, in turn, advance a loan to the Midland Railway Company!

There had, meanwhile, been several changes of plan in respect of the proposed alterations at Alcester. In essence, the Alcester Railway would converge with the existing Evesham & Redditch line at the north end of the station (as originally proposed), and the Midland Railway would extend the existing crossing loop northwards from the passenger station to meet the new line at Alcester Junction. There would thus be a section of double track between the junction and the station, with up and down running lines into and out of the platforms.

The existing three-siding goods yard would not be altered, but a long goods loop that already existed at the north end of the yard would be extended for a short distance and slewed to connect with the proposed new up line.

Earlier suggestions that a Great Western engine shed could be built in the Evesham & Redditch goods yard were abandoned, and instead a single-track structure would be constructed on Alcester Railway land to the north of the station. The new shed would be served by a long siding which, as initially proposed by William Clarke, would probably have formed a direct connection to and from the Evesham & Redditch goods yard; if constructed in this way, it would have been possible for terminating branch trains to have run onto Alcester Railway property via the Evesham & Redditch goods yard and sidings without entering the main line.

The difficulties that had apparently arisen at Alcester over the matter of the Alcester Railway and its relations with the Evesham & Redditch company had, by this time, been going on for several months and, possibly in an attempt to resolve the problems, James Allport, the MR General Manager, was now personally involved. In a letter addressed to William Clarke, the General Manager suggested that GWR engines should gain access to the shed by means of a direct connection from the Alcester Railway, but this course of action was disliked by the Great Western because of the different gradients and levels that would be involved.

Meanwhile, a contract for construction of the engine shed had been awarded to Messrs Scott & Edwards at a cost of £733 19s. 4d., and it would appear that the building was under construction while arguments about means of access were being continued.

It was eventually agreed that the connection between the shed road and the running lines would be at the point suggested by James Allport, and for this reason a crossover was laid between the branch and the engine siding, its pointwork being controlled from the nearby MR signal box. The position of the crossover was by no means ideal in that it necessitated a very short headshunt at the north end, with a disproportionately-long siding that extended southwards, through the engine shed, and then continued towards the MR goods yard and the site of the originally-proposed connection. Examination of the maps and photographs provided in Chapter Five will reveal that, for all intents and purposes, the resulting arrangement was the opposite of that suggested by William Clarke, the implication being that the shed, as finally built, was back-to-front!

As far as the station itself was concerned, the final agreement included provision for separate Great Western and Midland staff, and for this reason the Evesham & Redditch station building was enlarged to provide room for two staffing establishments.

There were no special additions to the existing goods yard, and earlier suggestions that an engine turntable should be installed were left in abeyance.

Once these contentious matters were finally settled, a formal working agreement was drawn up for the working and management of Alcester station. As four companies were involved, this was a quadripartite agreement, in which the roles of the two owning companies (the Evesham & Redditch Railway and the Alcester Railway) and the two operating companies (the GWR and the Midland Railway) were carefully defined.

It was agreed that the GWR and the Alcester Railway Company would pay the Midland Railway an annual rent of £150 for the use of Alcester station, while the Midland Railway and the GWR would share the cost of working and maintaining the station in proportion to their respective traffic.

The GWR and the Alcester Railway were, in return, allowed to use the station and its booking offices, sidings, junctions, cranes and other facilities, and run over the line between Alcester Junction and Alcester station with their locomotives and rolling stock. Furthermore, they would also be at liberty to 'place their own clerks, officers and servants' in the station, while the Midland Railway agreed to 'afford all necessary facilities and accommodation for such clerks, officers and servants at and in such station'.

The Midland Railway undertook to complete all necessary junctions, additions and alterations before 31st December 1876, including 'all proper locking apparatus' at the station and junction. All of this work would, however, be paid for by the Alcester Railway Company.

The most complex part of the quadripartite agreement concerned the system of cross-payment alluded to above, by means of which the money paid to the Midland Railway by the Alcester company would technically be a loan, upon which the MR would pay 5 per cent interest. The Evesham & Redditch Railway, meanwhile, would be paying £100 per annum to the Alcester Railway as stipulated in Clause 8 of the agreement:

'The Evesham Company shall pay to the Alcester Company half-yearly on the thirtieth day of September and the thirty-first day of March in every year the sum of one hundred pounds or such further sum as they shall deem fit, and also interest at the rate of five pounds per centum per annum on the balance from time to time due and owing in repayment of the sum advanced by the Alcester Company for additions and alterations...until the whole of such sum so to be advanced is repaid.'

In a further complication, Clause 9 of the quadripartite agreement provided for the payment of interest by the Alcester Railway Company to the Evesham & Redditch company:

'The Alcester Company shall after the opening of the Alcester Railway for public traffic pay to the Evesham Company interest at the rate of five pounds per centum per annum on the equal moiety of the cost of the alterations and additions of the Alcester station provided for in the third article of this agreement, such payment to be made in two equal half-yearly payments.'

It will be seen that the underlying purpose behind these financial provisions was a sort of cost-sharing exercise and, on reflection, one must conclude that this solution was probably the best deal that could be arranged between the four companies – all of whom must have recognised that the Alcester Railway would be bringing extra traffic to the existing Evesham & Redditch station.

OPENING OF THE ALCESTER RAILWAY

Having reached agreement with the Midland Railway, the Alcester Railway directors were, at long last, able to prepare for the public opening of their new line. Before this could take place, it was necessary for the railway to be inspected by the Board of Trade and 'passed' for the carriage of public traffic.

William Clarke was instructed to prepare the line for its inspection, and on 24th August 1876 he was able to report as follows:

> 'The works upon the main line and the alterations and additions at Bearley Junction have for some time past been completed.
>
> 'The necessary extensions at Alcester station and the junction there are being carried out by the Midland Railway. The engine shed, tank and roads upon the company's property and Alcester Junction are in a forward state.
>
> 'Colonel Hutchinson has been appointed to inspect the line on the 25th instant.'

The Board of Trade inspection took place as arranged on Friday 25th August 1876, the Inspecting Officer being Colonel C. S. Hutchinson of the Royal Engineers, on behalf of the Board of Trade. The Inspector was accompanied by various officials including William Clarke, the Company Engineer, the Earl of Yarmouth MP, Mr Edwards of Messrs Scott & Edwards, and officials of the Great Western and Midland Railway companies.

A contemporary press account in *The Redditch Indicator* recorded that 'a minute inspection of the entire line took place, and it was passed in every way satisfactory'. The paper added that the new railway would, when opened, afford 'facilities for reaching Stratford, Warwick and Leamington'; upon completion of the inspection, continued the paper, lunch was taken at Bearley, the food and refreshments having been prepared by 'Mr Hemming of the Swan Hotel, Alcester'.

The Alcester Railway was opened for public traffic on Monday 4th September 1876, this historic event being celebrated by the local populace in the usual way. A special train was run through to Leamington and, 'notwithstanding the unfavourable state of the weather', the Great Day was marked by a public luncheon in the Swan Hotel, Alcester, with the customary toasts and congratulatory speeches.

SOME DETAILS OF THE LINE

The new railway was a single-track, standard-gauge line running from Bearley Junction to Alcester Junction, a distance of 6 miles 40 chains. An intermediate station was provided at Great Alne, and this was the only station owned by the Alcester Railway Company – the junction stations at Bearley and Alcester being the property of the Stratford-upon-Avon Railway and the Evesham & Redditch Railway companies respectively. Trains ran through from Bearley station to Alcester station, a total distance of 6 miles 69 chains (as originally calculated), eastbound workings between Alcester and Bearley being regarded as 'up' services, whilst those proceeding in the opposite direction were considered to be 'down' workings.

The line was laid with flat-bottomed rail supplied by the Rhymney Iron Company Ltd, and conventional wooden cross sleepers were used throughout. There were no intermediate crossing places.

As eventually built, the line had four road overbridges and two road underbridges, together with two river bridges across the rivers Alne and Arrow. There were two gated level crossings, only one of which (at Great Alne) was over a public road. The other crossing carried a private road from Great Alne to Spencer's Mill across the line, and this had replaced a proposed road overbridge following an agreement between the railway company and local landowners whereby the road in question was discontinued as a public road, so that a level crossing could be substituted.

Ironically, the most impressive engineering structure along the route from Bearley to Alcester was the Edstone canal aqueduct, which predated the Alcester Railway by no less than 60 years. This structure, which crossed the line between Bearley and Great Alne, was owned by the GWR, having been part of the former Oxford Worcester & Wolverhampton Railway when that company was amalgamated (as the West Midland) with the Great Western in 1863.

The line was worked as simply as possible by train staff without tickets, and for this reason only one train was allowed on the route at any one time.

All train services were worked by the GWR under the terms of the operating agreement that had earlier been agreed. The original train service comprised six workings in each direction, at least one of which was a mixed passenger and freight working. In reality this service was soon found to be more frequent than was actually needed, and the timetable was soon reduced to just five trains each way.

The line was, from its inception, more successful than perhaps might have been expected, the receipts for the half-year ending 30th June 1877 being £1,222. When working expenses payable to the Great Western, station charges and other payments were deducted from this total, a balance of £803 was left and, with £63 brought forward from the previous year, £866 was available to pay the necessary interest charges and other expenses payable under the various agreements that had been made with the connecting companies. These additional payments totalled £404, but this still left the sum of £462 available for the payment of dividends, and it was, in consequence, agreed that a dividend of 1s. 8d. per ordinary share would be paid, leaving £45 to be carried forward.

THE END OF LOCAL CONTROL

With the railway in operation, the local traders and landowners who had helped to bring the line into existence saw no need to retain their interests in perpetuity, and it was therefore decided that the Alcester Railway would be sold to the GWR and the Stratford-upon-Avon Railway which already owned half of the shares. This amalgamation would be accomplished with the assistance of the Great Western company, the necessary powers being included in a General

Purposes Act which the GWR intended to obtain in the near future.

Until that Act could be secured, the Alcester Railway remained in being as an independent concern with its own directors. At the time of opening in 1876 the Alcester Railway's directors were Sir Charles Alexander Wood, William Bevington Lowe, John Kirshaw and William Spencer; the Chairman was still The Earl of Yarmouth. The officers included Secretary John C. Bull and Solicitor John L. Jones, whilst the Engineer was, of course, William Clarke.

Most of the directors and officers were locally-based, John Kirshaw, John Bull and John Jones being from Warwick, while William Lowe's address was given as Eatington, near Stratford-upon-Avon. William Spencer, who does not seem to have been one of the original promoters, was associated with the Spencer family who operated Great Alne corn mill. He left the board in 1877 and was replaced, as a director, by Captain Thomas Bulkeley (1807–1882) of Clewer Lodge, Windsor.

The appearance of Captain Bulkeley was highly significant. Like Sir Charles Alexander Wood, he was a long-standing GWR director and a close friend of Sir Daniel Gooch, the Great Western Chairman. The Alcester Railway was now virtually part of the Great Western, and final absorption was now little more than a formality.

On 22nd July 1878 the Alcester Railway Company was dissolved under the provisions of the Great Western Railway Act 1878, and the company was then vested jointly in the GWR and Stratford-upon-Avon railway companies, these being the owners of all of the capital of the Alcester company. A joint committee for the management of the vested Alcester Railway undertaking was set up, but this was really little more than a formality in that the Stratford-upon-Avon Railway was itself amalgamated with the GWR under the terms of a further Act obtained by the Great Western Railway on 20th August 1883. This provided for the amalgamation of the two companies with effect from 1st July 1883, and from that date the last vestiges of local autonomy were abandoned.

By these means, the GWR acquired full control of the former Alcester Railway and all its assets, and this obscure Warwickshire line thereby became another Great Western Railway branch line.

Great Alne station in 1889, with a group of local residents awaiting the arrival of the next train. This is the earliest known photograph taken of the line. The siding point rodding and signal wires led to a lever frame situated behind the photographer. The frame is believed to have been resited opposite the siding pointwork during siding alterations in January 1908. The wooden-posted oil lamps were replaced with standard GWR cast-iron lamp posts by c.1905 whilst the flat-bottom track survived until the lifting of the line during the Great War.
GREEN-JAQUES COLLECTION

CHAPTER THREE

THE LINE IN OPERATION (1883–1939)

THE Great Western takeover in 1883 made very little difference to the Alcester branch which had, from the time of its opening, been worked by the GWR as part of the GW company's extensive system; in practice, most regular travellers would probably have been unaware that a change of ownership had in fact taken place.

Traffic over this very rural Warwickshire line was modest in the extreme, and in Victorian days local travellers were offered an exceedingly sparse train service of just five workings in each direction between Bearley and Alcester.

The March 1884 timetable provides a useful glimpse of the pattern of operation in force during the late 19th century. In the up direction, trains left Alcester at 8.30 a.m., 9.45 a.m., 11.25 a.m., 2.45 p.m., and 5.55 p.m., whilst in the reverse direction the balancing down services departed from Bearley at 9.05 a.m., 10.55 a.m., 1.30 p.m., 4.45 p.m. and 7.10 p.m. Two up and two down workings ran as 'mixed' formations that conveyed both passenger vehicles and goods stock, and there was, in addition, provision for a 'ballast' train that ran as required on Mondays to Saturdays; there was no Sunday service, and indeed Sunday trains never became a feature of Alcester branch operations.

The 'ballast' train left Bearley at 12.00 p.m. and arrived at Alcester by 12.50 p.m. The return working left Alcester at 12.55 p.m. and arrived back in Bearley by 1.15 p.m.; it is assumed that this 'as required' service would have conveyed any additional coal or mineral traffic that was available.

The single line was, at that time, still worked by train staff without tickets with only one train on the line at any one time. There were, of course, no intermediate crossing places, though trains could if necessary cross at Bearley or Alcester.

This basic service of five passenger or mixed trains in each direction plus one ballast working as required persisted, with only minor alterations, throughout the 19th and early 20th centuries, the timetable for October 1894 being very similar to its 1884 predecessor.

In June 1895, daily operations began at around 8.00 a.m., when the duty train crew began preparing the branch locomotive for its day's work. The engine would have been in steam when the train crew turned up at Alcester shed, the usual practice being for a 'night fireman' to turn up during the early hours of the morning to clean the fire and replenish the engine's coal supply, so that it was ready for operation at the start of the following morning.

Having moved their locomotive from its shed to pick up the waiting train, the crew then propelled the engine and auto-trailer into the passenger station, ready to work the first up service to Bearley at 8.30 a.m. Reaching the latter station at 8.50 a.m., the branch train returned to Alcester at 9.00 a.m. with a mixed working, and at 9.30 a.m. the next up working departed from Alcester. The returning down service was another mixed formation, which reached Alcester at 11.00 a.m.

Operations continued with further up workings from Alcester at 11.20 a.m., and 2.02 p.m., the latter train being run as a mixed service. The 2.02 p.m. ex-Alcester reached Bearley at 2.22 p.m., and there was, thereafter, a long break in the train service until the departure of the 4.58 passenger service to Alcester. If, however, there was sufficient traffic, the 'as required' ballast train was run from Bearley to Alcester at 2.30 p.m., with a return trip at 3.25 p.m.

The final up train left Alcester as a mixed working at 6.02 p.m., the returning down service from Bearley back to Alcester at 7.59 p.m. being run as a purely passenger service.

A substantially-similar timetable was in force in 1908, and this provided up trains from Alcester at 8.22 a.m., 9.53 a.m., 11.25 a.m., 2.09 p.m. and 6.02 p.m., with corresponding return workings from Bearley at 8.57 a.m., 10.36 a.m., 1.05 p.m., 5.00 p.m. and 6.44 p.m. There were no Sunday services.

There had been a modest improvement by September 1913 in that the basic daily service was now six trains each way, with up workings from Alcester at 8.20 a.m. 9.33 a.m., 11.18 a.m., 2.05 p.m., 6.05 p.m. and 7.30 p.m., and balancing down trains from Bearley at 8.57 a.m., 10.43 a.m., 1.17 p.m., 5.00 p.m., 6.53 p.m. and 8.18 p.m. As in previous years, two up and two down trains were mixed passenger and goods services, and there were no advertised Sunday workings.

The branch from Bearley to Alcester was probably at its most profitable in the years between 1900 and 1914. Passenger booking for the entire branch (including Bearley) amounted to 28,090 in 1903, falling very slightly to 25,016 by 1913. In other words, the Alcester branch was carrying around 26,000 passengers per annum during the early 20th century, with total receipts of about £6,740 a year from all sources of traffic.

THE NORTH WARWICKSHIRE LINE

At the end of the 19th century the Great Western Railway initiated an ambitious programme of new route construction with the aim of providing alternative shorter routes to many of its existing main lines. One of these so-called 'Cut-Off' schemes was the Cheltenham & Honeybourne Railway which, with the connecting North Warwickshire line from Tyseley (some three miles to the south of Birmingham Snow Hill) to Stratford-upon-Avon, would create a new route from Birmingham to Gloucester and the south-west.

Although this new scheme was designed primarily to enable the GWR to compete with the rival Midland

The branch train alongside the down platform at Alcester in 1901 together with the loco crew, guard and a station porter. Even by this time the use of a single bogie brake third sufficed for the meagre traffic. The locomotive, '517' class 0–4–2T No. 203, was built in 1876 and was one of the type favoured for use on the line because its light axle loading and short wheelbase made it ideal for use on the lightly laid trackwork. This immaculate finish would have been the pride of the Alcester shed staff. No. 203 is known to have been in regular use on the line between 1901 and 1904. It was subsequently transferred to the Worcester and Leominster districts, ending her days at Oxford before withdrawal in April 1920.
COLLECTION G. D. BRAITHWAITE

THE LINE IN OPERATION 1883–1939

A general view of Bearley station taken c.1905, showing the station master's house alongside the approach road from the Birmingham to Stratford road. Having walked up the approach road, travellers finally reached platform level via a short flight of steps, which joined the up platform at the east end of the station building. There was no means of access from the back of the building and, in order to reach the booking office, passengers had to walk along the platform to enter the booking hall from the front.
LENS OF SUTTON

The approach to the aqueduct from Bearley during the 1900-05 period featuring the Bearley distant and the lie of the land before the construction of the North Warwicks line.
G. M. PERKINS

Railway route between Birmingham and Gloucester, it also served a useful purpose in that the 'North Warwickshire Line' between Tyseley and Stratford would open up a new suburban district to the south of Birmingham.

Powers for the Birmingham, North Warwickshire & Stratford-upon-Avon Railway were first obtained, by local interests, on 25th August 1894, but on this occasion the project was opposed by the GWR on the basis that the original proposal was a potentially-competing route that would harm Great Western interests. A few years later, however, a modified North Warwickshire scheme was proposed, and having obtained its Act on 9th August 1899, the new scheme was taken up by the Great Western; after further deviations had been suggested, the Great Western started work on the North Warwickshire line in 1905, and rapid progress was soon being made.

This new line was destined to have important consequences for the Alcester branch in that, when complete, the North Warwickshire route would intersect with the Alcester line at a point just 45 chains from Bearley station. A junction, to be known as Bearley North Junction, would be established at this point, and the North Warwickshire line would then continue southwards to converge with the Stratford-upon-Avon line at a second new junction to be known as Bearley West Junction.

The line from Bearley North Junction to Bearley West Junction was brought into use in May 1907, and Alcester branch trains were temporarily diverted onto this new route while engineering work proceeded on the original Alcester Railway route between what now became Bearley East Junction and Bearley North Junction. While this work was under way, it was necessary for branch trains to start their journeys by setting off along the Stratford-upon-Avon line as far as Bearley West Junction where they reversed and, after proceeding along the newly-built North Warwickshire line to Bearley North Junction, they were able to rejoin their own line for the rest of the journey to Alcester.

This temporary arrangement lasted for only a limited period, and when the necessary track and signalling work was completed, the branch trains were diverted back onto their original route. On 9th December 1907 the North Warwickshire line was opened for goods traffic, whilst passenger workings began using the new line on 1st July 1908.

Bearley North Junction, showing the Alcester branch proper diverging from the North Warwicks line and passing beneath the Edstone or Bearley Aqueduct c.1907. This picture was taken from a point close to the Bearley–Aston Cantlow road underbridge, which was situated immediately behind the photographer. Notice the lower repeater arms on the bracket signal on the right provided for sighting purposes through the arches of the aqueduct. This lofty signal was about 50ft in order that it could be seen from a distance above the aqueduct. It was eventually replaced by a tubular-post ordinary single-arm home signal some 15ft high c.1952. G. M. PERKINS

Bearley North Junction signal box was opened on 9th December 1907 when the North Warwicks line opened for local goods traffic between Tyseley and Bearley West Junction. Local passenger services commenced on 1st July 1908. This picture, taken facing Bearley West Junction in 1908, also shows the Alcester branch engine with her crew, and in the signal box windows, the telegraph operator and the signalman. The building behind the engine was a fogman's hut. G. M. PERKINS

THE LINE IN OPERATION 1883–1939

This view, taken looking across the top of the aqueduct towards Stratford c.1908, shows the towpath edged with cast-iron railings. The Alcester branch stop signal can be seen in the background together with the new PW hut, which replaced an earlier one sited on the opposite side of the branch. By the early 1930s, this building was replaced by a similar hut located between the branch and the up running line of the North Warwicks line.
G. M. PERKINS

Perhaps one of the best known features of the GWR Alcester–Bearley branch was the use of the Bearley Aqueduct for the purpose of watering the branch engine. This well-known photograph, by the railway enthusiast and historian G. M. Perkins from Henley-in-Arden, is believed to have been taken in 1903 and shows the branch engine (an unidentified 517 class) taking water from the aqueduct. The fireman is seen on the ladder with his hand on the valve wheel. Two minutes were allowed in the working timetables for this operation. The panel of corrugated iron placed behind the wood-encased pipe was probably some form of protection against the elements; no fire-devil would appear to have been provided during the early years. The picture predates the construction of the North Warwicks line. The Bearley distant signal can be seen in the distance.
G. M. PERKINS

This picture of Alcester station was taken looking towards Evesham c.1903-05 and shows the original station signal box at the end of the down platform. The accommodation within the main station building was, from left to right: general waiting room, ladies room, booking hall and ticket-office cum through passageway, with the MR station master's domestic accommodation beyond. There was a separate section inside the booking office area for issuing GWR tickets.

LENS OF SUTTON

THE LINE IN OPERATION 1883–1939

The ramifications of this new route to Birmingham were quite substantial as far as the Alcester branch was concerned. By the end of 1905 Tyers No. 6 tablet instruments were installed between Bearley station and Alcester Junction signal boxes coupled with the occupation key system with six intermediate key boxes for the use of the Permanent Way Department. Perhaps most importantly, the branch became part of the new line for a short distance in the vicinity of Bearley North Junction, and this entailed the creation of two block sections (Alcester Jcn.–Bearley North and Bearley North–Bearley East) instead of the one long section between Bearley and Alcester, as had originally been the case.

Confusingly, the imposition of the North Warwickshire line created two possible datum points for calculating dis-

A general view of Alcester station, facing Redditch c.1906-08, with a southbound MR freight headed by a Kirtley 0–6–0 tender engine. The newly installed station signal box was erected in connection with signalling alterations in December 1905. LENS OF SUTTON

A group of Alcester station staff photographed probably c.1910-14, with both the MR and GWR station masters present. The MR station master seated in the centre was probably Mr. Kilby.
COLLECTION R. S. CARPENTER

Spencer & Son's covered wagon and three-horse team making their way through the long ford near Little Alne c.1900.
THE OLD GREAT ALNE VILLAGE BOOK COLLECTION

This picture, taken around the turn of the century, shows local farmers' carts laden with sacks of corn awaiting their turn to be unloaded at Spencer's Mill. THE OLD GREAT ALNE VILLAGE BOOK COLLECTION

This Foden steam lorry belonged to Spencer, Son & Hancox and is seen here alongside the gates at Spencer's Crossing c.1910.
THE OLD GREAT ALNE VILLAGE BOOK COLLECTION

Another Edwardian period postcard view of Great Alne taken c.1910 and clearly showing the platform-mounted corrugated-iron goods shed provided in the 1908 alterations to the goods yard accommodation.   COLLECTION R. S. CARPENTER

tances on the former Alcester Railway, and whereas the original (and historically-correct) datum point had been Bearley station, the new, post-1908 starting point became Bearley North Junction. This resulted in a situation in which timetable distances were usually calculated from the start of the journey at Bearley, while engineering department distances were invariably taken from Bearley North Junction.

The *Table 3* will help to explain this anomaly:

TABLE 3

	Distance from Bearley	Distance from North Junction
Bearley Station	00m 00ch (Datum 1)	00m 00ch
Bearley East Junction	00m 07ch	00m 00ch
Bearley North Junction	00m 45ch	00m 00ch (Datum 2)
Aston Cantlow Halt	02m 09ch	01m 44ch
Great Alne station	04m 29ch	03m 64ch
Alcester Junction	06m 51ch	06m 06ch
Alcester station	06m 71ch	06m 26ch

WORLD WAR ONE AND ITS AFTERMATH

In retrospect there is general agreement among railway historians that the Edwardian period marked the very zenith of the Railway Age. In those halcyon years before 1914, great railway companies such as the Midland Railway and the GWR held an undisputed monopoly of land transport. Railways were at the 'leading edge' of Britain's world-beating industrial technology and, at a time when rural communities such as Great Alne and Aston Cantlow moved at the speed of a horse, the familiar steam railways – which now reached into every corner of the land – were the fastest, safest and most efficient means of transport on earth.

It was indeed a golden age, and in the long, hot summer of 1914, most people must have imagined that the railways, like the British Empire, would last for evermore. Sadly, that illusion of permanence was shattered when the Imperial German Army marched into the tiny, inoffensive and neutral country of Belgium, and in response to this brutal action Britain immediately declared war on the aggressors. The United Kingdom thereby became involved in a major European conflict after a hundred years of peace, and the 'Golden Age' of railway transport was brought abruptly to a close.

With motor transport still in its infancy, the railways were needed to rush men, horses and equipment to the front, and the whole system was placed on a war footing in August 1914. Government control was enforced from the very start of the conflict, a Railway Executive Committee being formed to direct railway operations on the British mainland

THE ALCESTER BRANCH

(the Irish lines were not brought into Government control until 1917).

Some lines were needed for the war effort, but other routes – especially those such as the Alcester line which were well away from areas of military or industrial activity – were subjected to various economies in order that vital resources could be concentrated on more important wartime routes.

Although railwaymen were exempted from conscription when that measure was introduced in 1916, large numbers of men from the Great Western (and other companies) volunteered for service in HM Forces. This placed even greater strains on the railway operating departments and, as the war continued without sign of abating, the need for ever-greater economies became clear. As far as the Alcester branch was

This picture of Alcester was taken on 21st September 1920 during the period when the branch was closed as a result of the Great War, and before the track was relaid during the autumn of 1922.
R. K. COPE

The Alcester road bridge seen from near the loco shed at Alcester, looking towards Bearley during the 1917-23 temporary closure. Note that the junction pointwork for the branch was left in situ during this period as was the MR signal post formerly used for controlling trains approaching from Bearley. G. M. PERKINS

This picture, taken on 21st September 1920, shows Great Alne station during the period of temporary closure resulting from the Great War. As well as the recovery of the track, the corrugated-iron goods shed on the platform had also been removed for use elsewhere on the GWR system. It is believed that the station house continued to be occupied during this period. R. K. COPE

THE LINE IN OPERATION 1883–1939

Bearley station, facing east towards Hatton c.1920-22. Note the absence of Alcester on the station nameboard.　　STATIONS UK

concerned, this process began with the closure of Alcester locomotive shed with effect from 1st November 1915, followed by the withdrawal of passenger and freight services from the entire branch with effect from 1st January 1917. The track was removed shortly after for further use elsewhere.

At this point the story is extremely vague in that the track removed from the branch between Bearley North Junction and Alcester is said to have been requisitioned for military use and sent to France; however, legend has it that the vessel carrying this equipment was torpedoed in the English Channel and sent to the bottom, taking rails and other railway equipment with it! Tales of British ships being lost in the English Channel while loaded with railway equipment are strangely persistent. Trackwork from the GWR Uxbridge High Street branch, for example, is supposed to have been lost on a torpedoed ship in the early months of 1917, whilst a similar fate is said to have met the Bideford Westward Ho! & Appledore Railway's track and locomotives on a mysterious vessel known as the SS *Gotterdammerung*. Similarly, permanent way material from the Caledonian Railway's Inchture Tramway is said to have been lost at sea while en route to the Western Front in 1917.

Alcester, Westward Ho! Uxbridge and Inchture are widely-scattered places at opposite ends of the country, yet stories of railway equipment being lost at sea in or around March 1917 are told independently in all of these locations. There is thus some corroborative evidence to support the theory of a catastrophe in the English Channel at that time. Furthermore, it is known that enemy U-Boat activity reached record levels in the early months of 1917, over 881,000 tons of shipping being lost in April 1917 alone.

With strict censorship in force, the true facts were never entirely clear. Locomotives, permanent way equipment and other materials were being sent all over the world by 1917,

Another photograph taken during the 1917-23 closure, this time from the road overbridge at 1 mile 34¼ chains, looking towards Bearley on 21st September 1920. Notice that the telegraph poles and wires were left in situ.　　R. K. COPE

and it is more than likely that some, at least, of the trackwork removed from the Alcester branch found its way to France.

The Great War ended on 11th November 1918, but the railways remained under Government control until 1921. There was, by this time, much debate about the role of the railways in the postwar era, and it was eventually decided that the main-line companies would be 'grouped' into four large, regionally-based undertakings, this government-directed course of action being seen as an alternative to outright nationalisation. Accordingly, on 1st January 1923, the 'Big Four' railway companies were created under the terms of the Transport Act 1921.

The Great Western Railway retained its identity after the 1923 Grouping, but the Midland Railway – which impinged upon the Alcester branch at its western end – became part of

Great Western Railway

ON AND FROM

Wednesday, August 1st, 1923,

THE LINE BETWEEN

Great Alne & Alcester

WILL BE

RE-OPENED

FOR PASSENGER, PARCELS AND GOODS TRAFFIC.

THE PASSENGER TRAIN SERVICE WILL BE AS UNDER:—

WEEK-DAYS ONLY.   RAIL MOTOR CAR (ONE CLASS ONLY).

		a.m.		a.m	a.m.	a.m.	p.m.	p.m.	p.m.	
LONDON (Paddington)	dep.	12A15	..	6 30	9C 10	10C40	12 50	2C10	4 10	..
LEAMINGTON SPA	,,	8 10	..	9 55	10 50	12 45	2 32	4 5	5 55	..
BEARLEY	arr.	8 40	..	10 18	11 15	1 11	2 59	4 39	6 26	..
BIRMINGHAM (Snow Hill)	dep.	7 33	..	9 25	10 15	11X19	2 7	4 0	6P 7	..
BEARLEY	arr.	8 31	..	10 7	11 15	12X42	2 59	4 39	7 6	..
STRATFORD-ON-AVON	dep.	8 43	..	—	11 45	—	2 26	3 25	6 45	..
WILMCOTE	,,	8 51	..	—	11 52	—	2 33	3 32	6 52	..
BEARLEY	arr.	8 55	..	—	11 56	—	2 36	3 35	6 56	..
		a.m.		a.m.	p.m.	p.m.	p.m.	p.m.	p.m.	
BEARLEY	dep.	9D 3	..	10 38	12 20	1 20	3D23	4 55	7 7	..
ASTON CANTLOW HALT	,,	9D11	..	10 44	12 26	1 26	3D31	5 1	7 13	..
GREAT ALNE	,,	9D17	..	10 50	12 33	1 32	3D39	5 8	7 19	..
ALCESTER	arr.	9D24	..	10 58	12 40	1 39	3D46	5 15	7 25	..
		a.m.	a.m.			a.m.	p.m.	p.m.	p.m.	p.m.
ALCESTER	dep.	7 57	9 30	..	..	11 18	12 50	2D 5	4 0	..	5D40
GREAT ALNE	,,	8 12	9 37	..	..	11 25	12 57	2D15	4 7	..	5D50
ASTON CANTLOW HALT	,,	8 18	9 43	..	..	11 31	1 3	2D23	4 13	..	5D58
BEARLEY	arr.	8 24	9 49	..	..	11 37	1 9	2D30	4 19	..	6D 5
BEARLEY	dep.	8 40	10 8	..	..	12 43	1 11	3 0	4 41	..	6 13
WILMCOTE	arr.	8 46	10 12	..	..	—	1 15	3 4	4 45	..	6†30
STRATFORD-ON-AVON	,,	8 52	10 17	..	..	12 50	1 20	3 9	4 50	..	6 20
BEARLEY	dep.	8 40	—	..	..	11 45	..	2 50	5 31	..	7 20
BIRMINGHAM (Snow Hill)	arr.	9 17	—	..	..	12 32	..	3 52	6 57	..	8P20
BEARLEY	dep.	8 56	10 50	..	..	11 57	..	2 38	5 31	..	6 56
LEAMINGTON SPA	arr.	9 20	11 17	..	..	12 25	..	3 5	6 5	..	7 22
LONDON (Paddington)	,,	11 0	1 25	..	..	2 5	..	5 0	8 5	..	10 0

A Mondays excepted.   C Slip Carriage   D Mixed Train.   P Moor Street Station.   X On Saturdays
Birmingham depart 12.25 p.m., Bearley arrive 1.10 p.m.   † Bearley depart 6.26 p.m.

2.31 p.m. and 7.57 p.m. Trains from Wilmcote to Stratford-on-Avon will be discontinued.
3.10 p.m. Stratford-on-Avon to Wilmcote will be discontinued.

For further information application should be made at the Stations; or with regard to Passenger and Parcels Traffic to Mr. A. BROOK, Divisional Superintendent, G.W.R., Birmingham, or to Mr. R. H. NICHOLLS, Superintendent of the Line, G.W.R., Paddington, W.2; and in reference to Goods Traffic to Mr. J. H. GALLIMORE, District Goods Manager, G.W.R., Worcester, or MR. E. LOWTHER, Chief Goods Manager, G.W.R., Paddington, W.2.

PADDINGTON STATION,   **FELIX J. C. POLE,**
July, 1923.   *General Manager.*

THE LINE IN OPERATION 1883–1939

a new organisation known as the London Midland & Scottish Railway.

RE-OPENING OF THE LINE
Meanwhile, the abandoned line from Bearley to Alcester had not been re-opened, and local traders and residents began to fear that the branch would never be reinstated. At length, following vigorous protests from the inhabitants of Alcester and the presentation of a petition from local residents, the Great Western agreed to re-open the line. The campaign to save the branch had been orchestrated by Doctor Richard H. Spencer, a local medical practitioner who worked at the Hertford Memorial Hospital, Alcester, while at about the same time the inhabitants of Aston Cantlow were able to persuade the GWR that a small station or halt beside the junction of the roads from Bearley to Little Alne and Aston Cantlow would be a viable proposition that would bring extra traffic to the railway.

The line from Bearley to Alcester was relaid as cheaply as possible with secondhand permanent-way materials, and on 18th December 1922 the section from Bearley North Junction to Great Alne was re-opened for passengers and goods traffic, the Electric Train Tablet instruments being temporarily set up at Great Alne to facilitate this initial reinstatement.

A few months later, on Wednesday 1st August 1923, the remaining portion of the branch between Great Alne and Alcester was re-opened for passenger and goods traffic, with an improved train service of seven trains in each direction, two up and two down services being mixed passenger and freight trips.

The re-opened branch was laid with inside-keyed bullhead rail in lengths of about 30ft. The chairs were attached to the sleepers by oak trenails and iron spikes, oak keys being used to secure the rails to their chairs. The track was bedded down in ashes supplied from the local GWR engine sheds, with clinker placed at the bottom and finer ashes on top.

At Great Alne, the track layout was similar to that provided prior to closure, and the branch was signalled much as it had been before 1917, with one long block section between Bearley North Junction and Alcester worked by Electric Train Tablet.

As before, the line was worked as simply as possible with just one train and no crossing loops, though up and down workings were able to pass at Bearley and Alcester.

The single line was controlled by Electric Train Tablet instruments at Alcester and Bearley North Junction signal boxes, all intermediate siding connections being controlled by ground frames. A further ground frame was brought into use at Spencer's Crossing, which was also equipped with a 'crossing indicator' instrument. A telephone circuit linked Bearley North Junction Box, Spencer's Crossing, Great Alne and Alcester.

Telephone and Electric Train Tablet Occupation Key Boxes were restored for the use of the permanent way department between Bearley North Junction, Great Alne and Alcester.

In its revised form the branch was equipped with up home and inner home signals at Bearley North Junction and down home and distant signals at Alcester. The up branch distant at Bearley North Junction was fixed at danger. Elsewhere, there were working distant signals on either side of Spencer's Crossing, together with distants on each side of Great Alne level crossing. Interestingly, the new signals provided at the time of the 1922–23 re-opening were mounted on concrete posts – apparently due to timber shortages during and after the Great War.

Track relaying staff on an earlier operation at Great Alne in 1912.

THE ALCESTER BRANCH

The long hoped-for stopping place at Aston Cantlow had been authorised by the GWR on 1st June 1922 at an estimated cost of £327. It was opened, as an unstaffed halt, on Monday 18th December 1922, when the first section of the line was brought back into use.

The newly re-opened branch was worked entirely by push-pull auto-trains, a significant feature of the revised timetable being an increase in frequency from six to seven daily workings. In the up direction, trains left Alcester at 7.57 a.m., 9.30 a.m., 11.18 a.m., 12.50 p.m., 2.05 p.m., 4.00 p.m. and 5.40 p.m., whilst in the down direction the corresponding workings left Bearley at 9.03 a.m., 10.38 a.m., 12.20 p.m., 1.20 p.m., 3.23 p.m., 4.53 p.m. and 7.07 p.m.; two of the up and two of the down services were mixed workings that conveyed both passenger vehicles and goods rolling stock.

POSTWAR PROBLEMS AND THE 1925 BRANCH LINE SURVEY

Although the GWR had retained its identity as a result of the 1923 Grouping, the 1920s were a time of change and uncertainty. The years following the 1914–18 war were characterised by a slump in industrial activity which was harmful to the railways in that it caused a drop in revenue. At the same time, wage inflation had started to have an adverse effect on barely-profitable lines such as the Alcester branch, while the war years had greatly assisted the infant road transport industry by producing large numbers of improved motor vehicles, many of which subsequently came onto the secondhand market at minimal prices.

Road transport, in fact, posed a major threat to the very existence of all rural branch lines; millions of former servicemen had flooded onto the labour market after the recent war, and many of these men used their service gratuities to set themselves up as self-employed bus or lorry operators. Road transport offered ample opportunities for small-time businessmen without formal qualifications to make good profits and, whereas licensing restrictions were so lax that the new road hauliers could pick and choose their freight, the railways – as common carriers – were obliged by law to carry *all* types of goods traffic, even if such traffic was unprofitable. In truth, the 1920s were the heyday of the 'cowboy' road transport operator, and in these circumstances the railways were faced with severe competition for both passenger and goods traffic – especially in rural areas in which road vehicles could fully utilise their greater flexibility of operation.

Aston Cantlow halt was constructed largely from old sleepers and provided with a standard GW-pattern corrugated-iron waiting shed and four oil-lit lamps. This picture was taken on 18th May 1930.
CLARENCE GILBERT

The branch auto-train approaching Alcester station, the single auto-trailer being propelled by an unidentified '517' class 0-4-2 tank, in summer c.1928.
ALCESTER HISTORICAL SOCIETY

Faced with these problems, the Great Western decided to carry out a detailed survey of its rural branch lines in 1925. In general, the survey was designed to identify where savings could be made, one of the options to be examined being outright closure of the least profitable routes. The Alcester branch was one of over 50 lines included in the survey – although in this case the GWR was unable to reach a firm conclusion. The information obtained was, nonetheless, of considerable interest. It transpired that the daily train service of six auto-car trips each way consumed 32.2 lbs of coal per mile, and when the cost of fuel was added to the estimated track maintenance and renewal costs of 18.15d. per mile for passenger trains and 20.52d. per mile for freight workings, the line's running costs totalled £3,064 per annum.

For the purposes of the survey, the 'Alcester Branch' was defined as the line from Bearley North Junction to Alcester, and on this basis the wage costs for the branch amounted to £1,148, while the cost of clothing, fuel, water stores and rates, etc., added another £2,650 to the annual expenditure (this included payments of £842 made to the LMS Railway for the use of Alcester station). The total annual expenditure on the Alcester branch came to a grand total of £6,862, and this figure was set against annual receipts for the year 1925 of £8,852. The branch was, on the evidence of these figures, running at a profit of £1,990.

Other information revealed in the report concerned the type and quantity of goods traffic that was being handled on the branch. The principal sources of traffic were said to be 'coal, round timber and roadstone', and in 1925 the line had carried 7,205 tons of coal and minerals and 5,657 tons of general goods traffic.

As far as traffic receipts were concerned, the figures were as shown in *Table 4*.

TABLE 4

Station	Passengers	Parcels	Goods	Total Receipts
Great Alne	£323	£54	£2,717	£3,094
Alcester (including Aston Cantlow)	£1,231	£143	£4,384	£5,758
TOTALS	£1,554	£197	£7,101	£8,852

Although these figures may seem surprisingly modest, the overall results of the 1925 survey were regarded as satisfactory, and there was no question of any case being made for closure at that time. On the other hand, there appeared to be little scope for the implementation of any further savings, and to that extent the survey may be said to have had a negative result.

On a footnote, it should perhaps be pointed out that the Alcester branch was not, by any means, the least profitable GWR branch in the 1925 survey. The Yealmpton branch, for example, was found to be running at a loss of £2,071, while the Pontrilas and Hay line was losing £3,826 per annum. On the other hand, although the Alcester branch was not actually running at a loss, its operating profits were hardly spectacular, and for that reason the longer-term future of the line did not look particularly good.

LOCOMOTIVES AND ROLLING STOCK

Little is known about the locomotives employed on the Alcester to Bearley branch during the earliest years of its life, although, by analogy with neighbouring Great Western lines, it would probably have been worked mainly by four-coupled '517' class engines from the Victorian period onwards. These 0-4-2 tank engines were designed by George Armstrong and built at Wolverhampton, the first batch appearing as saddle tanks in the 1860s. From 1870 the original engines were rebuilt (with extended wheelbases) as

Views of Bearley station are not easy to find. This one, facing Hatton during 1933, features a glimpse of the goods yard and the goods shed behind the up platform. The main station building immediately beyond dated from about 1875, when the Alcester Railway Company provided enlarged passenger accommodation. The structure by the Alcester Company's Engineer, William Clarke, was to a standard design which he also used on a number of other small railway companies' lines on which he was employed. The waiting room on the down platform would appear to have dated from the opening of the station, as did the goods shed, with its rather large opening for rail access, serving as a reminder of the broad-gauge era of the Stratford-on-Avon Railway Co. The building was equipped with a 1-ton crane inside. The cattle pen, just discernible in front of the goods shed, was constructed from old bridge rails on a red-brick base. The siding adjacent to the line serving the goods shed was generally reserved for the local coal merchants, the local traders' wagons in evidence here belonging to Stevens, Bretnall & Kelland, Haunchwood, and Stevco. The stacking ground area of the yard can be seen in the left-hand corner of the photograph.
P. A. HOPKINS

side tanks, and renumbered from 517 onwards; as such they became part of the well-known '517' class, which remained in production until 1895.

The engines built as side tanks had 16in × 24in cylinders and 5ft 2in coupled wheels, and these dimensions became standard for the entire class after the original 0–4–2STs had all been rebuilt to conform with the 0–4–2Ts.

Over the years various '517' class engines worked on the Alcester branch, the engines concerned being sub-shedded in the branch shed at Alcester, where their green livery, tall parallel chimneys and polished brass domes contrasted with the usual Midland Railway classes on Ashchurch to Redditch services. Perhaps for this reason, the branch engine became known locally as 'The Coffee Pot', and in the fullness of time this appellation was applied to the train itself, so that local travellers might, for example, speak of 'going to Stratford on the Alcester Coffee Pot'!

One of the engines used on the line was '517' class 0–4–2T No. 203, which was at Alcester around 1900 but afterwards worked on the Wallingford and Blenheim & Woodstock lines. Sister engines Nos. 523, 1156 and 564 were also used at various times, while in the early 1920s the regular engine was No. 537. The latter engine seems to have remained at work on the branch for several years until its eventual replacement in the 1930s.

Small-wheeled 0–6–0 saddle tanks of the '850' and similar classes are said to have appeared sporadically on the Alcester line, and it is also possible that steam railmotors were employed on the route for a short period during the Edwardian period.

The normal branch train around 1910 appears to have been a mixed formation consisting of one long bogie composite vehicle and a short-wheelbase guard's vehicle, but following the introduction of push-pull 'auto-train' operation elsewhere on the GWR, auto trains were introduced on the Alcester branch, the regular '517' class 0–4–2Ts being adapted for push-pull working. Special auto-trailers were introduced at the same time, the most significant feature of these vehicles being the driver's compartment from which the train could be controlled while it was being propelled from the rear. (Some of these push-pull coaches were in fact former steam railmotor cars from which the powered bogie had been removed.)

In 1932 the Collett '48XX' class 0–4–2Ts were introduced as replacements for the veteran '517' class engines, and these new locomotives soon appeared on the Alcester branch, the regular engines being Nos. 4801 and 4848. The auto-trailers in use at this time were 70ft vehicles of various types, one of which was car No. 76, which was photographed at Bearley in 1937 behind Collett '48XX' 0–4–2T No. 4801.

Another auto-trailer know to have been used on the Alcester branch was car No. 78, which was rostered for work on the branch in September 1929. However, as the cars were changed for cleaning and maintenance once a week, others would doubtless appear from a 'pool' of passenger rolling stock used for local routes.

Nos. 76 and 78 were both 70ft trailers that had been built in 1911 as part of Lot 1190 (Diagram 'T'). On the days when the branch vehicles were changed, the incoming trailer

'Bulldog' class 4–4–0 No. 3449 Nightingale *of Worcester shed alongside Bearley East Junction Box c.1933, with a Worcester–Leamington vacuum fitted freight.*
P. A. HOPKINS

The 9.36 a.m. mixed train for Alcester awaiting departure from Bearley station c.1938. The autotrailer was No. 74 but the 48XX 0–4–2 tank is not identified. Goods vehicles were normally marshalled at the rear of mixed formations irrespective of the direction of travel, and thus a westbound mixed working such as the one depicted here is a 'sandwich' formation with the locomotive in the middle.
BERT BROMWICH, CTY. KIDDERMINSTER RAILWAY MUSEUM

would be worked southwards from Birmingham off the 1.20 p.m. Moor Street to Bearley service.

When mixed passenger and freight trains were run, a standard GWR 'Toad' brake van, branded for use on the branch, was used to provide brakes at the rear of the loose-coupled vehicles; when not in use it was usually left at the Bearley end of the line. Trains normally ran with the engine at the Bearley end and the passenger trailer at the rear, with any goods rolling stock on the mixed workings at the rear. An up, or eastbound, mixed train would therefore consist of the '48XX' branch engine, followed by the auto-trailer, perhaps half-a-dozen goods vehicles and the Toad brake van whilst in the down direction, the formation typically comprised the auto-trailer, then the engine (running bunker-first), followed by half-a-dozen or so goods vehicles and the brake van.

Incoming goods traffic included coal, grain, timber, general merchandise, sheep and cattle. By the 1930s, covered vans were being increasingly used for cattle cake, general merchandise, or other loads, whilst some grain was delivered in special Great Western 'Grano' vans. These vehicles looked rather like ordinary covered vans, and some even had side doors so that they could be used for general traffic as well as bulk grain. When carrying grain, they were loaded through sliding hatches in their roofs, and tiny glazed windows were inserted into their ends, so that railway staff could see if they were fully loaded. Such vehicles were occasionally seen at Great Alne in connection with grain traffic for Messrs Spencer Son & Hancox's mill, though ordinary open wagons were preferred for this traffic because they could more easily be unloaded by one man.

Cattle traffic brought Great Western 'Mex' cattle wagons onto the line, whilst Mex wagons also brought occasional loads of Welsh sheep to Great Alne. Timber consignments or other long or bulky loads were carried on GWR 'Macaw' single or bogie bolster wagons.

Coal was, in general, carried in privately-owned open wagons which bore the liveries of a variety of colliery companies or coal merchants; one of the local coal distribution firms were Messrs F. & G. Butler of Alcester, although details of their wagon livery are, as yet, unclear. Other locally-based coal dealers included Frank Hawkins, J. A. Bates and Fred Shrimpton, all of whom rented coal wharves in the goods yard at Alcester.

TOWARDS CLOSURE

The service of seven trains each way introduced immediately after the re-opening of the line was soon reduced to a basic pattern of six up and six down workings, but the introduction of a through working to Stratford-upon-Avon and back was warmly welcomed by local residents, who were thereby able to avoid the inconvenience of changing at Bearley.

Collett 0–4–2T No. 4801 is seen here in 1935 with the Alcester branch auto-trailer approaching some GWR box vans which were about to be coupled up in readiness to form a mixed train working to Alcester.   M. J. DEANE

A northbound express hurrying past Bearley North Junction, hauled by an unidentified 'Saint' class 4–6–0. This view, taken c.1933 from the Bearley aqueduct, shows the Alcester branch, which is seen diverging to the right. P. A. HOPKINS

Below: *'517' class No. 564 and the customary auto-trailer No. 76 passing Bearley North Junction on a Bearley-bound service c.1933. This photo was taken from the Bearley–Aston Cantlow road.*
P. A. HOPKINS

THE LINE IN OPERATION 1883—1939

The revised timetable was fully established by the later 1920s, the September 1928, July 1930 and July 1932 timetables all following a 'standard' pattern. The first up train left Alcester at 7.55 a.m., and at 9.35 a.m. worked back mixed from Bearley. At 10.15 a.m. the branch locomotive and auto-trailer set off on its daily through trip to Stratford, and having called at Great Alne and Aston Cantlow at 10.22 a.m. and 10.28 a.m. respectively, continued to its destination via Bearley North Junction, Bearley West Junction and Wilmcote, arriving in Stratford-upon-Avon at 10.42 a.m. It returned at 11.23 a.m. via the same route, Bearley station being omitted on both the outwards and return trips.

Thereafter, operations continued throughout the day, with up services to Bearley at 12.50 p.m., 2.05 p.m., 4.00 p.m. and 5.40 p.m. The 2.05 p.m. and 5.40 p.m. services both ran as mixed workings. In the down direction, the corresponding westbound services left Bearley at 1.20 p.m., 3.10 p.m., 4.57 p.m. and 7.07 p.m., the 3.10 p.m. working being

The tranquil setting of Great Alne station on 13th June 1934. The two LMS box vans in the sidings may well have been for Spencer's Mill. This picture makes a striking comparison with the scene of 1920. The bullhead-chaired track seen here was used over the entire length of the branch in the relaying.
L&GRP

A late 1930s view of Alcester station, with the Alcester branch auto-car standing in the yard. The engine may have been at the nearby GW engine shed between duties.
LENS OF SUTTON

'517' class 0-4-2 tank No. 1157 with the branch auto-trailer No. 76 awaiting departure from Alcester on 19th September 1935. Built in December 1875, No. 1157 lasted in service until November 1935, ending her days on the branch and the nearby Leamington–Stratford line. Notice the well-kept station garden behind the locomotive.
LENS OF SUTTON

This photo of Alcester station, taken from the down starting signal looking towards Redditch on 13th June 1934, features a departing LMS freight bound for Redditch. In the distance we can see the LMS 1932 replacement signal box and, beyond, the GWR engine shed can just be discerned to the left of the MR signal and goods train. L&GRP

The GWR Alcester branch brake van branded 'Bearley' No. 35860 features in this photo of the goods shed at Alcester c.1936-38. P. J. GARLAND

Collett 0–4–2 tank No. 4814 with a Stratford Mop Special mixed train at Bearley station c.1938. This was one of the rare occasions when corridor stock was used on the branch.
BERT BROMWICH, CTY. KIDDERMINSTER RAILWAY MUSEUM

THE LINE IN OPERATION 1883–1939

'517' class 0–4–2 tank No. 1157 at Stratford-on-Avon on an auto working from Alcester. This picture, taken on Saturday, 6th July 1935, just beyond the Alcester Road bridge, shows the train in the process of reversing into the up line platform in readiness to return to Alcester.
L. T. PARKER, CTY. AUDIE BAKER

a mixed train. There were no Sunday services, but a slightly modified service applied on Saturdays, when three of the six daily trains travelled through to Stratford-upon-Avon.

The Saturday train service underwent further modifications in connection with the annual Stratford-upon-Avon 'Mop Fair', which was held every year on two successive Saturdays in October. The annual 'Mop' was one of the largest such events in England, and it attracted people from miles around; on these occasions the normal branch train was strengthened by the addition of an extra third-class bogie vehicle for the afternoon through services to Stratford. In addition, a special late-night trip was run from Stratford to Alcester and, as might be imagined, a ride on the 'Mop Night Special' was a revellers' delight!

In physical terms, the Alcester branch changed very little after its re-opening in 1922–23, the one significant change carried out during the 1930s being the progressive renewal of the old-fashioned inside-keyed trackwork with its 30ft lengths of '86A' bullhead rail. The replacement '00' bullhead rail secured in outside-keyed chairs was laid on all curves as it was found that the old inside-keyed rail tended to 'spread' out of gauge as the sleepers became aged.

The relaying was carried out by about eighteen men, which was the number of people needed to lift and carry the replacement rails which were 44ft 6in long. The relaying gangs were taken to their work on the normal branch pumped trolley, which propelled an additional four-wheel trolley in front at a speed of about 15 miles per hour with six men pumping. Although the two vehicles were not coupled, loose planks laid between the pump trolley and the unpowered trolley were used to seat the men who were not needed to operate the pump mechanism, this weight apparently proving sufficient to keep the trolleys together.

Faced with falling levels of passenger and freight traffic at Great Alne and, to a lesser extent, at Alcester, the Great Western sought ways of reducing the cost of operating the branch. In practice, this was not an easy task because the line was already being worked as cheaply as possible by one push-pull train that shuttled up and down the 6¾ miles branch and, as we have seen, the route was maintained by a minimal number of permanent way men, although as yet there had been no real search for staff economies. In 1932, however, Great Alne was placed under the control of the Bearley station master, enabling the Class 5 post at Great Alne to be deleted, leaving a Grade 1 porter as the only member of staff there. In that same year, the Great Western station master's post at Alcester was dispensed with and the station was placed under LMS supervision.

Collett '48XX' class 0–4–2T No. 4816 with the evening mixed train, seen on arrival at Bearley on 2nd August 1938. The trailer was No. 76.

F. K. DAVIS

THE LINE IN OPERATION 1883–1939

The 5.45 a.m. Leamington to Honeybourne local freight, hauled by a pannier tank and seen here on the down line alongside Bearley East signal box during 1938. The shunter was Walter Morris. The up freight in the distance was waiting at signals. The junction for the North Curve can be seen in the middle distance, with the station goods yard on the right and the roadstone crushing plant beyond.
BERT BROMWICH CTY. KIDDERMINSTER RAILWAY MUSEUM

Following these economies, the branch was worked by just two people, apart from the train crews and permanent way men. The concept of 'basic railways' had not yet been developed, but the Alcester branch was, by the 1930s, probably about as close to it as the conditions of the time would have allowed. The two remaining members of staff had to be retained to work the two level crossings at Great Alne and Spencer's Crossing, and short of demoting the line to light railway status, it is hard to see how the GWR could have eradicated these gated crossings.

Despite these economies, by 1938 the line continued to run at a loss, although it may, to some extent, have fed traffic onto more viable lines such as the North Warwickshire route. One could speculate that if the GWR could have arranged the train service in such a way that travellers could have reached Birmingham from Alcester without changing en route at Bearley, there might have been an increase in traffic. But then, on the other hand, people wishing to travel to and from Birmingham could already do so by the LMS route via Redditch, and there was little incentive for the Great Western to compete for this traffic. Furthermore, road transport was proving far more attractive to many people.

This picture of ex-ROD 2–8–0 No. 3048, probably on a Banbury–South Wales ironstone train, shows the fireman about to surrender the single-line staff, c.1939. A. T. LOCKE
CTY. KIDDERMINSTER RAILWAY MUSEUM

Collett 0-4-2T No. 48144 with trailer No. 216 alongside the down platform at Alcester in September 1939 shortly before the GWR branch closed. Note the whitewashing of platform edges and doorways and the partial blacking-out of the station lamp to comply with wartime blackout regulations, etc.
J. E. NORRIS

CHAPTER FOUR
THE WAR YEARS

The familiar view of Great Alne station from the level crossing, this time c.1939 just prior to the closure of the branch. Note the removal of the poster boards and the whitewashed platform edging.   A. T. LOCKE, CTY. KIDDERMINSTER RAILWAY MUSEUM

ALTHOUGH road transport had threatened the Alcester branch since the First World War, the real and lasting damage did not begin to take effect until the later 1930s, when road hauliers captured much of the traffic that had hitherto been carried by rail. The effects, as far as Great Alne were concerned, can only be described as catastrophic, and by 1938 the station was only handling 386 tons of freight per annum. Ironically, whilst Bearley, in contrast, was enjoying a boom in freight traffic, this was mainly because the station was handling large quantities of road-building materials that would ultimately be used to help rival forms of transport.

Table 5 will reveal how much damage had been done in terms of lost traffic, and when it is remembered that the line's total receipts in 1925 were £8,852, the scale of the decline will become clear. The figures quoted relate to 1938, and they should be compared to those in *Table 4*.

TABLE 5

Station	Passengers	Parcels	Goods	Total Receipts
Great Alne (including Aston Cantlow)	£149	£11	£386	£546
Alcester	£481	£24	£1,032	£1,537
TOTALS	£630	£35	£1,418	£2,083

It was obvious that, by 1938, the Alcester branch was running at a loss, yet few people could imagine a day when the 'Coffee Pot' would no longer run through the pleasant Warwickshire meadow lands; it was assumed that railways were a vital part of the national infrastructure, and that they would be maintained in perpetuity, not only for social but also for strategic reasons at a time of growing national tension.

WORLD WAR TWO

The 1930s had been dominated by the rise of militaristic dictatorships in Italy, Germany, Spain and Japan. The people of these nations were told that Western democracies such as Britain and France were weak and decadent, whereas the newly revitalised, state-controlled regimes in countries such as Germany represented the forces of progress. As we now know, the rise of fascism led inevitably to a policy of aggressive nationalism; in the end, on Sunday 3rd September 1939, Britain declared war on Germany following that country's invasion of Poland, and thus – less than 21 years after the Great War – Britain and its allies were once more at war with Germany.

The development of new weapons of mass destruction such as aerial bombing and poison gas was thought to have transformed warfare out of all recognition, the consensus of opinion among 'experts' being that the outcome of this latest war with Germany would be decided by a series of so-called 'knock-out blows' in which great cities would be wiped out in a matter of days. Faced with this frightening scenario, the

Government commenced preparations for war months before the outbreak of hostilities, and detailed Air Raid Precaution (ARP) and evacuation plans had already been drawn up.

On 24th August 1939 the passing of the Emergency Powers (Defence) Act had prepared the way for government control of the railway system, and this measure was rapidly put into effect, the General Managers of the main-line railway companies and London Transport being formed into a Railway Executive Committee through which Government control could be enforced.

For ordinary travellers, the nightly ARP 'Blackout' and the sight of soldiers, sailors and airmen hurrying to join their ships or units served as reminders that there was a war on, but otherwise the first months of the war were so quiet that people began to speak derisively of a 'Phoney War'.

The timetable in force on the Alcester branch in September 1939 comprised the time-honoured service of six trains each way, with up trains from Alcester at 7.57 a.m., 10.22 a.m., 12.43 p.m., 2.02 p.m., 4.05 p.m. and 5.40 p.m., and down workings from Bearley at 9.36 a.m., 11.36 a.m., 1.15 p.m., 3.10 p.m., 4.45 p.m. and 7.32 p.m.

However, within weeks of the outbreak of war, the service was suspended as from the end of the summer timetable on 25th September 1939, and this effectively meant the closure of the Alcester branch.

To Bill Hunt – then a schoolboy staying in Great Alne – it seemed entirely appropriate that the end of the railway should have coincided with the start of the Autumn season, and his first-hand recollections of that fateful September capture something of the poignancy of the occasion:

> 'On Sunday 3rd September 1939 war was declared. Three weeks later, I was up at Great Alne at the home of a friend. His mother, a widow, was the local schoolmistress, the house lying not far from the railway line.
>
> 'On the other side of the line was the River Alne, and that afternoon three of us had spent our time on and about the water with my friend's folding canoe. We had done this most weekends that summer, but now Autumn was setting in – the day had been unsettled and the evening sky was gloomy, with a threat of rain. We had decided this would be our last afternoon on the river that year. As for next year, who could tell what was going to happen? There was a war on, as the saying went, but nothing terrible had yet taken place. Perhaps it would, after all, be over by Christmas – certainly some people professed to think so. But there was, nevertheless, a feeling of great uncertainty – we were entering *terra incognita*, where our maps of the future, so confidently drawn, did not seem any longer to correspond with the topography around us.
>
> 'Sitting in the schoolhouse that evening, we heard the branch train start up from Great Alne station, the beat of the engine getting louder as it neared. It whistled once, hauntingly, in the gathering darkness, passed the schoolhouse a field away, and went on towards Alcester, the so-familiar sound dying away on the wind.
>
> '"Well", said Mrs Mahoney, "there goes the last Coffee Pot". I had not, until that moment, heard that we were to lose our favourite train. (The GWR, of course, must have relished the excuse of wartime economy to withdraw it since it was certain it had run at a loss for years.) I was not, in those days, a railway enthusiast, but trains were among the things I liked, and they were so established as a part of life that it seemed obvious that they were going to be there for ever. The Coffee Pot, on which I had personally journeyed hardly a dozen times, was particularly dear to me, and I felt sad and disorientated at the news of its cessation.'

As the withdrawal of train services between Bearley and Alcester (exclusive) was, technically, a suspension, there remained a possibility that the branch would ultimately be re-opened, although, of course, the 38-chain west curve between Bearley East and Bearley North junctions remained open for unrelated passenger and freight services between Birmingham Moor Street and Bearley.

The so-called 'Phoney War' lasted for several months, and this unexpected respite enabled ARP wardens and other services to continue their training for the aerial bombardment that was expected to come. In nearby Coventry, the 'Battle for Production' was already being waged, and by 1940 the city was heavily involved with aircraft production, wheels, tyres, radio sets, artificial fabrics, aircraft engines, airframes and magnetos being among the many vital components that were being manufactured in great quantities.

The earlier fears of a 'knock-out blow' had not been forgotten, and in anticipation of the cataclysmic destruction that was still being predicted, stockpiles of fuel, food and other items were rapidly assembled. By the Spring of 1940 the Alcester branch had been pressed into use for the storage of coal wagons, and the whole line was soon crammed with a continuous string of spare vehicles that extended for almost the entire length of the route. Photographs taken at the time suggest that these were mainly older-type private-owner wagons that were being held in reserve as replacements for possible war losses elsewhere.

The sudden and unpredicted fall of France in May and June 1940 enabled the Germans to concentrate their full attention on the United Kingdom and, in anticipation of imminent invasion, the British Government ordered that all road signs and station nameboards should be taken down. The first bombs fell in the Coventry area in June 1940, and between 18th August and the end of October the city was attacked on seventeen occasions, over 198 tons of bombs being unleashed on this important industrial target, resulting in 856 casualties, including 176 killed.

As the bombing campaign intensified, with major raids on London, the RAF began to retaliate with raids on German cities; on 8th November the British bombed Adolf Hitler's favourite city of Munich, which was widely regarded as the birthplace of the Nazi movement. This led directly to 'Operation Moonlight Sonata', in which 450 Luftwaffe bombers attempted to wipe out the City of Coventry in a concerted night attack.

This raid, which was the first of its kind on a provincial city, took place on the night of 14th–15th November 1940, and by the following morning many of the city's vital factories had been put out of action. Over 60,000 buildings had been damaged or destroyed, and 568 people had been killed. Although the scale of the destruction was far less than had earlier been predicted, the Coventry air raid caused severe fires that lit up the night sky for miles around, and could be clearly seen in places as far away as Rugby, Alcester and Birmingham; the detonation of high-explosive bombs was felt in Stratford-upon-Avon, almost 20 miles away.

THE WAR YEARS

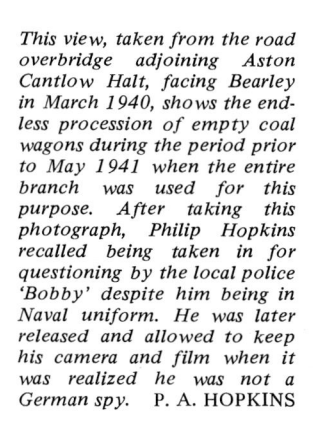

This view, taken from the road overbridge adjoining Aston Cantlow Halt, facing Bearley in March 1940, shows the endless procession of empty coal wagons during the period prior to May 1941 when the entire branch was used for this purpose. After taking this photograph, Philip Hopkins recalled being taken in for questioning by the local police 'Bobby' despite him being in Naval uniform. He was later released and allowed to keep his camera and film when it was realized he was not a German spy. P. A. HOPKINS

One of the industrial plants that had been damaged in the raid was the Parkside factory of Maudslay Motors Ltd; it was reported that machines had been damaged and 'all work stopped'. More seriously, Coventry's essential services were more or less out of action and with no water, power or telephone system it was very difficult for production to be immediately resumed.

With the fear of more raids, the Maudslay Motor company was moved to the grounds of the manor house at Great Alne as part of a policy of dispersal. The new site was far from any other major targets, and partially hidden by woodland, which offered an ideal opportunity for camouflage against air attack.

THE 'SECOND RE-OPENING' OF THE BRANCH

The new premises were taken over in February 1941, and work on the new factory was soon under way, but as most of Maudslay's key staff lived in Coventry, some 25 miles away, and petrol rationing was strictly in force, suitable road transport could not be arranged. However, following representations from Maudslay Motors, it was decided that the Alcester branch should be re-opened for passenger traffic between Bearley and Great Alne.

The first machines in the factory were working by July or August 1941, and many workers were soon travelling to and from their homes in Coventry, on an unadvertised workmen's train which was run to and from Great Alne. The initial service – which possibly commenced as early as May 1941 – was apparently worked by an LMS railmotor set throughout from Coventry to Great Alne, but by June 1941 a GWR auto-train was in use between Leamington Spa and Great Alne.

Precise details of the LMS push-pull set are elusive, but it is thought that the train involved may have been a two-coach set worked by an auto-fitted ex-London & North Western Railway tank locomotive. The original service worked from Coventry to Leamington Spa, calling at Kenilworth; after reversal at Leamington, the train travelled to Great Alne via Warwick, Bearley East Junction and Bearley North Junction.

These arrangements were short-lived, and they were soon replaced by two separate services, the LMS train running over the Kenilworth line to Leamington LMS station, while the Great Western connecting service ran to and from the adjacent GWR station to Great Alne. No timings are shown in the GWR Working Timetable for 6th October 1941, but there is a note to the effect that 'Workmen's trains worked by auto-engine operate Bearley North Junction (from and to Leamington Spa) and Great Alne'.

As part of wartime economies the electric train tablet working was withdrawn and instead 'one engine in steam' with a wooden train staff was introduced between Bearley North and Great Alne from Monday, 18th May 1942.

The 5th January 1942 Working Timetable reveals that the morning service left Leamington Spa at 7.32 a.m. (weekdays) and, having called at Warwick and Aston Cantlow at 7.37 a.m. and 8.00 a.m. respectively, it reached Great Alne by 8.05 a.m. The engine was then booked to return light to Leamington (arr. 8.58 a.m.), from where it returned at 2.15 p.m. to work the 6.08 p.m. up service from Great Alne to Leamington Spa. The train called at Aston Cantlow (6.13 p.m.) and Warwick (6.36 p.m.) on the return journey, with an arrival time at Leamington Spa of 6.40 p.m.

On Saturdays, the locomotive was booked to return light from Leamington Spa at the earlier time of 2.15 p.m., and it then worked a 3.10 p.m. (SO) service from Great Alne to Leamington Spa. This pattern of operation was clearly arranged to suit the needs of Maudslay's staff, many of whom travelled all the way from Coventry (though others had found safer accommodation in the surrounding towns and villages – hence the intermediate stops at Warwick and Aston Cantlow).

This evocative wartime photograph shows horse-ploughing in progress alongside the Alcester–Great Alne section of the branch near Kinwarton c.1940-45. Note that all the stored wagons visible were private owner colliery or coal trader wagons.
COLLECTION R. S. CARPENTER

THE WAR YEARS

This unadvertised workmen's service remained unchanged throughout 1943, but a May 1943 working notice shows that the down service from Leamington Spa was then leaving at the slightly earlier time of 7.30 a.m. on weekdays, with an arrival time at Great Alne of 8.03 a.m. At 8.18 a.m. the '48XX' 0-4-2T engine returned to Leamington as before, but on Tuesdays and Fridays it took the auto-trailers with it; on Mondays, Wednesdays and Thursdays, however, it returned light engine. At 5.05 p.m. the engine (or engine and trailers on Tuesdays and Fridays) worked back to Great Alne and at 6.03 p.m. (12.00 p.m. on Saturdays) the up service returned to Leamington Spa.

The coaches used on these workmen's trains were usually older type trailers, one having shoulder-height partitions between the compartments while the other was an open saloon with seats around the sides. Two of the regular wartime travellers were Jack Sidwell and Arthur Hinks, and they recalled that there was a distinct 'community spirit' aboard the trains, with singing, dancing and a regular card school!

The trains would sometimes be held up at Bearley or Hatton as a result of air raids or other 'incidents' further up the line and, as on other wartime trains, the ARP blackout was strictly enforced, with dimmed interior lighting and window blinds for use at night. Stations, too, were barely lit, with perhaps one or two heavily-shaded platform lamps near any barrow crossings, and white edges to the platforms to prevent people from falling onto the line. People who travelled throughout from Coventry to Great Alne were faced with a long and tiring day, particularly so for those who, on arrival at Coventry in the middle of a winter's night, had to cycle back to their homes through the blacked-out streets.

On one occasion, the engine hauling the trains became derailed at Great Alne, but after much effort by the footplate crew and the Maudslay workers themselves the locomotive was coaxed back onto the rails.

Jim Castle was a senior porter at Leamington Spa during the early 1940s, who acted as guard on the passenger service between Bearley and Great Alne. Jim recalls:

'I lived in Henley in Arden and cycled from there to Leamington, leaving home at about 6.30 a.m. and booked on at 7.15. My first duty was to act as guard on the 7.30 a.m. to Great Alne. The passengers on this train came from Coventry and worked for Maudslay who had set up a factory about half a mile from Great Alne station.

'They arrived at 7.20 and walked from the Avenue station under the foot tunnel to the down bay where we were waiting with our 48XX tank (leading) and one auto-car.

'We had about sixty passengers when I first worked the service – mainly men – later there were women too as the wartime work increased. I never had to check tickets, it being part of a contract job – I suppose they showed their IDs at Coventry.

'On arrival at Great Alne and after passengers had left, the fireman used the key on the end of the staff to unlock the ground frame and the coach was set back to the yard loop where it was left for collection in the early evening. Incidentally, the loop had evidently been relaid or repaired to allow this. I understood the coach we had came up from the West Country where it had become spare – it was the only autocoach we had at the time and remained at Leamington until after the war. I heard it said it later went to the Severn Valley area.'

Jim returned with the driver and fireman on the light engine.

'On arrival back at Leamington I relieved the ticket collector for his breakfast break and worked as required. Later in the day, I was the guard of the 1.30 p.m. to Stratford and took my bike with me. I came back with a Stratford guard on the return trip and left the train at Bearley to cycle home for my break. Later I cycled to Great Alne and worked the 6.0 p.m. train back to Leamington, the loco for which had come out light to collect the coach.

'On arrival at Leamington at 6.30, the workers returned to the Avenue station where they caught a train home at 6.40. While the coach was waiting to be worked back to the sidings, I had already collected my bike, booked off and began my cycle home.'

It is not known who worked the service before Jim, but early in 1944 'a Ruth Cuss took my place – she later married an American soldier and I never heard any more of her.'

The Maudslay factory was in full production by the Autumn of 1942, by which time a group of traders in the Great Alne area had asked if the railway could be used for freight traffic. In September 1942 it was agreed that a twice-weekly freight service would be operated in conjunction with the scheduled Leamington Spa to Stratford-upon-Avon pick-up goods working.

Peter Chater, who was a fireman at Leamington shed 1942–1954, remembers working the Leamington–Stratford Goods. 'On the return journey, usually on a Friday, we would work a trip from Bearley to Great Alne with three or four wagons of coal. The porter from Bearley came with us to open the gates at Spencers Crossing and assist with shunting. The line was quite overgrown in places with overhanging vegetation and quite a lot of wildlife was disturbed. Normally the Stratford Goods was worked with a 51XX 2-6-2T or a 66XX 0-6-2T. But if a trip to Great Alne was required then a 57XX 0-6-0T was provided.

The inwards freight conveyed to Great Alne by this revived freight service was chiefly coal for Maudslay's works and domestic purposes. Meanwhile, the westernmost section of the branch between Great Alne level crossing and Alcester remained closed and was still being used for wagon storage, which produced further movements of spare or crippled stock along the eastern part of the branch.

The wartime passenger service continued throughout the summer of 1943 and into the following year, a note in the May 1944 GWR Working Timetable suggesting that the emergency service of one down and one up passenger train was still in operation, worked by an 'auto-engine and trailer stabled at Leamington Spa' on weekdays only. However, the service finally ceased with effect from 3rd July 1944, when buses were used to take the Maudslay workers to and from Great Alne. Furthermore, the conveyance of coal supplies for the Maudslay works was also switched to road haulage in 1945 to avoid double-handling at Great Alne station. However, this did not mean the end of the line because significant quantities of sugar beet were being sent from the station during the season for use in a sugar refinery at Kidderminster.

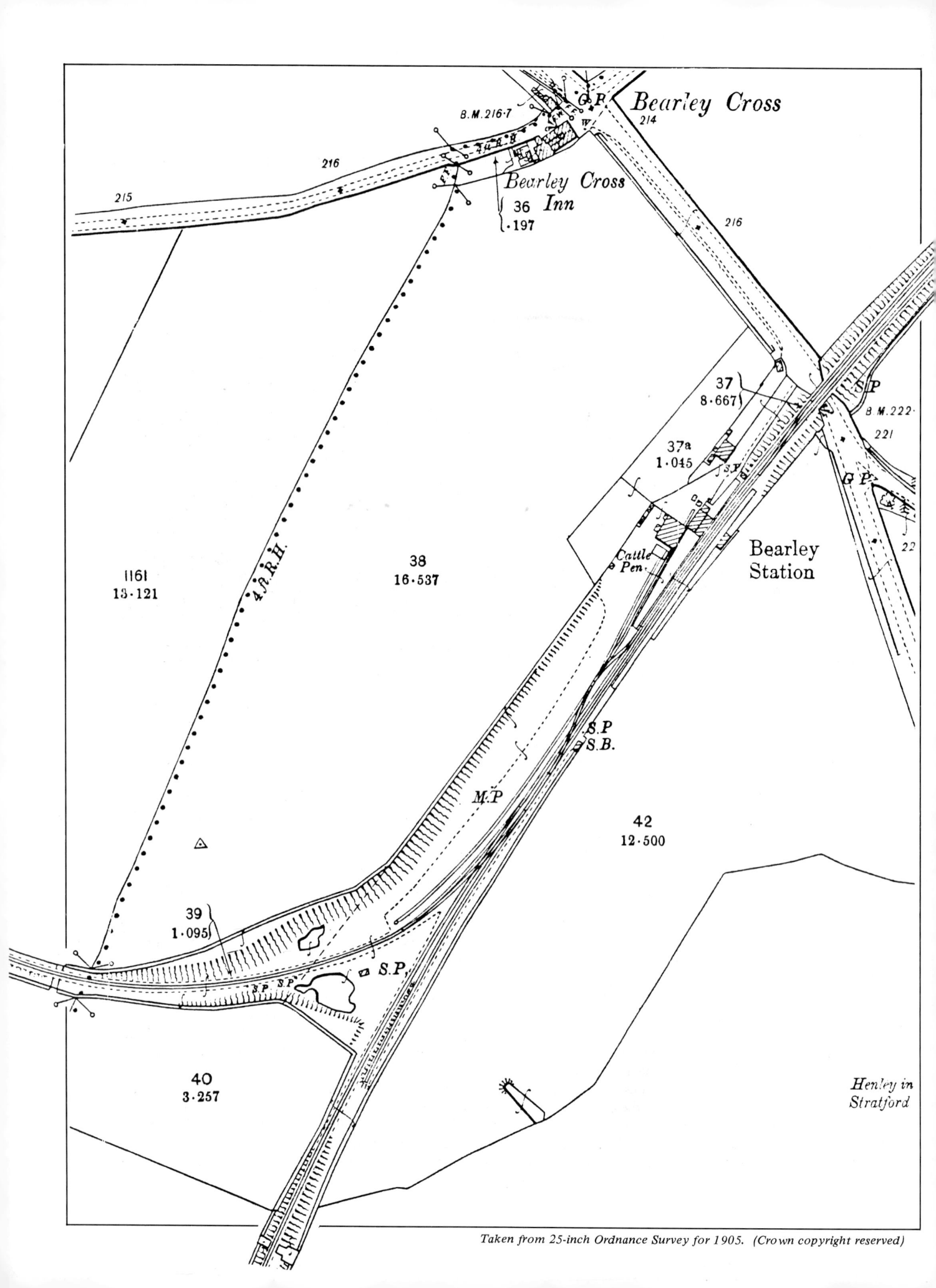

Taken from 25-inch Ordnance Survey for 1905. (Crown copyright reserved)

CHAPTER FIVE

THE LINE DESCRIBED

BEARLEY STATION

A morning scene at Bearley station on Thursday, 16th September 1937, showing No. 4801 and the Alcester branch auto-trailer No. 76, which had probably just arrived. Both 4801 and trailer No. 76 were regularly used on the branch during the late 1930s. In the background it is just possible to make out the small stone-crushing plant which was based in the yard at this time to process quantities of stone chippings which were despatched by rail for road-making purposes. The crushing plant had vanished by the early 1950s. R. J. BUCKLEY

BEARLEY station is situated on the GWR line from Hatton to Stratford-on-Avon, about half a mile to the east of the village of Bearley. It is set amidst the open farm land and tree-lined hedgerows that typify this part of Warwickshire. When first opened on 10th October 1860, this railway was a mixed-gauge single line extending from a junction on the Birmingham–Oxford line at Hatton station to a terminus at Birmingham Road, Stratford, a distance of 9¼ miles, with intermediate stations at Claverdon, Bearley, Wilmcote and Stratford-on-Avon. Following connection with the OW&W Railway line from Honeybourne in 1861, narrow-gauge services were run through to Honeybourne and Worcester.

During the 1860s, Bearley station was a quiet country station with a crossing loop, a signal box, two brick-faced platforms, a modest-sized goods yard, goods shed, weighbridge and office and a station master's house, all constructed in red brick, with slate roofs. The original station building may well have been a brick-built structure in keeping with the adjoining stations at Claverdon and Wilmcote, but this was demolished in 1876 when Bearley became a junction for the Alcester Railway. This resulted in alterations which included the provision of a new station building on the up side or eastbound platform and a smaller waiting room on the down side.

The new station building was designed by William Clarke, the Alcester Company's engineer, and was constructed of red brick, with a gabled, slate-covered roof in a style employed on other lines for which he was responsible, including the Newent Railway, the Ross & Ledbury Railway, the Bristol & North Somerset Railway and the Leominster & Kington Railway.

When the North Warwickshire line was opened in 1907–8, part of the existing line between Wilmcote and a point south of Bearley was incorporated into the route and consequently doubled. The divergence of the new route involved the creation of a new junction, named Bearley West, to the south of the station and another two to the west of the station, Bearley North and Alcester Branch Junction, where the new line joined, then left the route of the existing Alcester branch. The existing junction at the station for the Alcester branch was renamed Bearley East Junction; at the same time the line between the West Junction and the East Junction was doubled, and a new connection from the down line to the goods siding was put in, as was an additional siding in the goods yard. The station remained in this form through to the end of the 1930s when the layout was subject to yet more upheaval.

In the Edwardian period, Bearley typically issued around 14,000 tickets per annum. In 1903, for example, the station booked 14,551 tickets, whilst in 1913 there were 14,359 passenger bookings. These annual figures had fallen to around 10,000 bookings a year during the 1920s, although there

49

were, by that time, between 130 and 190 season ticket holders making regular journeys to and from the station. In 1937 Bearley issued 8,534 ordinary tickets, but there were also 301 season ticket sales, suggesting that the station had developed a healthy commuter business by the later 1930s.

Freight traffic amounted to about 5,000 tons per annum during the early years of the 20th century, and this figure remained more or less constant throughout the 1920s. Thereafter, the amount of freight traffic handled increased considerably, and in 1938 Bearley dealt with 18,690 tons of freight. By this time, the development of railway-owned road delivery vehicles meant that certain stations gained extra traffic while others declined as their 'smalls' traffic was diverted to selected railheads and country lorry centres.

A view from the new footbridge, showing the temporary connections laid in during the initial stages of the new works in March 1939.
A. T. LOCKE, CTY. KIDDERMINSTER RAILWAY MUSEUM

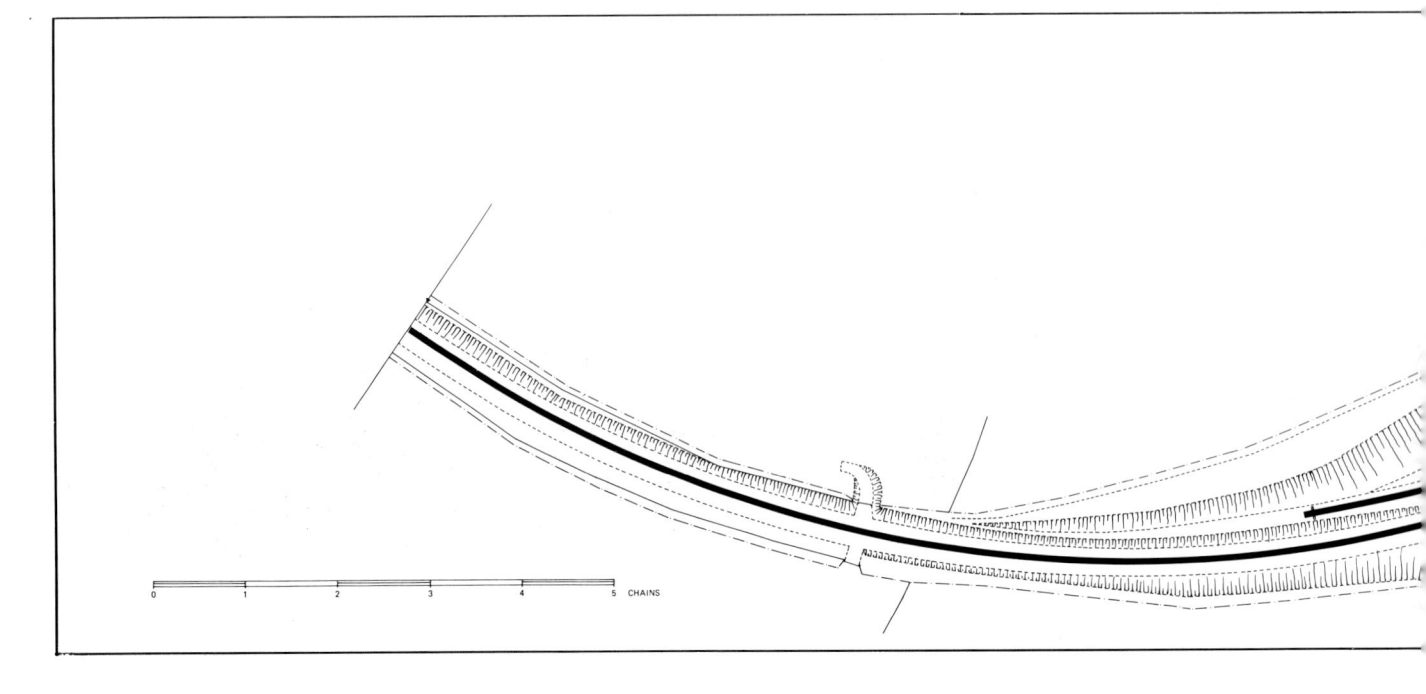

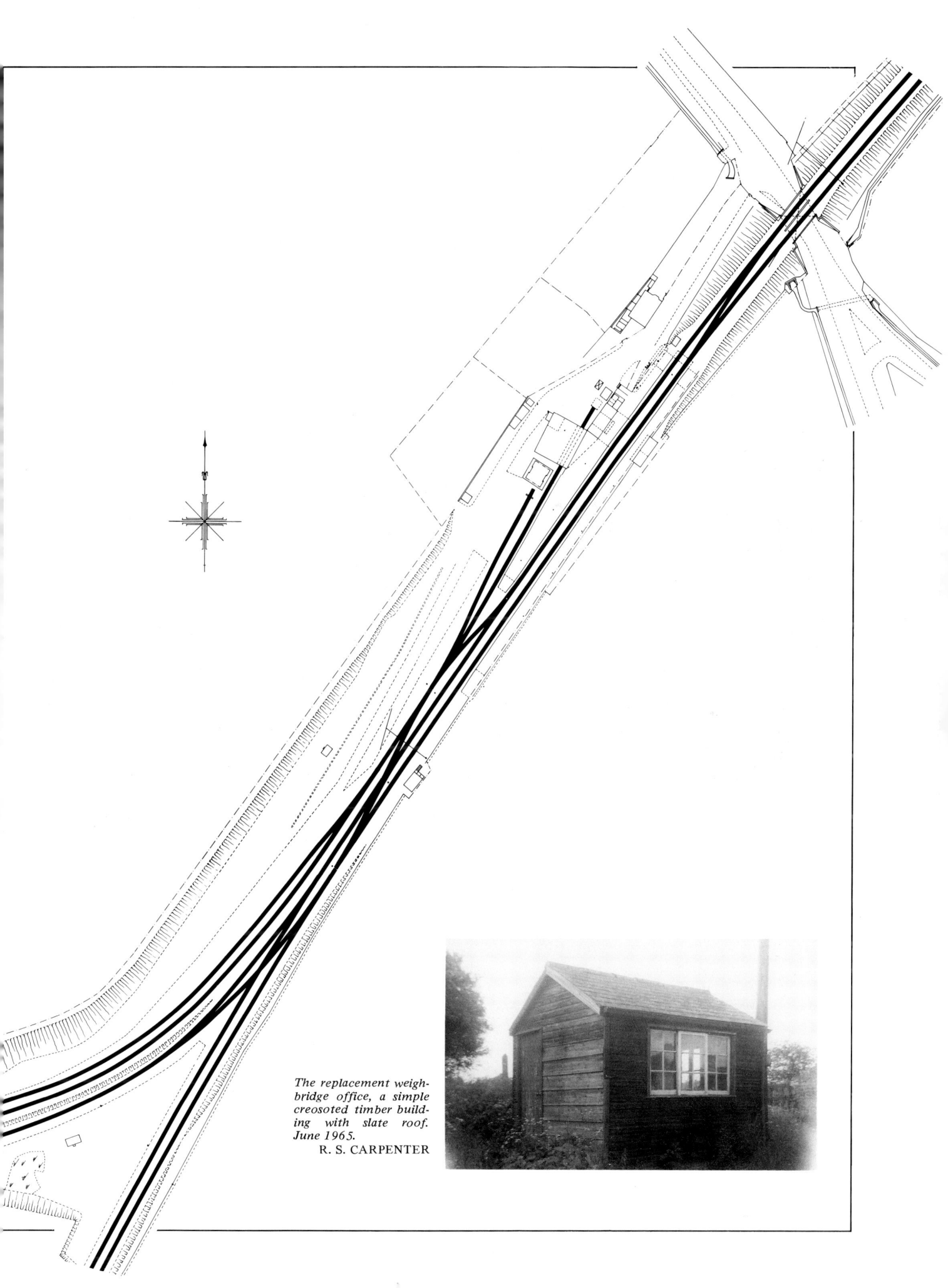

The replacement weighbridge office, a simple creosoted timber building with slate roof. June 1965.
R. S. CARPENTER

The station building on the left was a small, rectangular, brick-built structure, with a low-pitched gable roof and a projecting platform canopy. Internally, it contained three main rooms: from left to right (when looking at the building from the platform) these were the booking office, waiting room and ladies' waiting room respectively. A small extension at the east end contained a porters' room cum store, together with the gentlemen's lavatories, the latter being at the rear. The platform canopy, which incorporated a section of glazing, was supported on ornamental brackets bearing the initials 'SR' rather than GWR, the building being the property of the Stratford-upon-Avon Railway Company. The canopy was edged with tongue-and-groove fretwork, this type of ornamentation being associated particularly with lines engineered by William Clarke. During 1938, work commenced on the Hatton–Bearley widening, which included a certain amount of station alterations at Bearley. When this view was taken on 19th May 1939, the alterations had already been completed, and involved extending the platforms at the Hatton end of the station, the addition of a footbridge, and the rebuilding of the waiting room on the down platform. Even after rebuilding, the overall appearance of this small structure was entirely traditional; the saw-tooth awning was of GWR design, and in this respect the down side building was in contrast to its counterpart on the up side. The down side building incorporated a small staff room at its west end. By this date, new signalling was also being erected, i.e. the replacement Up Starter at the far end of the platform extension, seen with the 'X' on its arm, which denoted that it was not in use.

NATIONAL RAILWAY MUSEUM

THE LINE DESCRIBED

This picture, also taken on 19th May 1939, features the Alcester branch auto, which can be seen alongside the up platform. At this time the trackwork had yet to be altered, the down refuge siding (its catch points and the running line disc signal) becoming the down running line in due course. Prior to 1939, the only means of access between the two platforms had been by a wooden barrow crossing at the east end of the station. Another improvement carried out at that time concerned the provision of electric lighting.

NATIONAL RAILWAY MUSEUM

The rear elevation of the main station building in June 1965, showing the original Stratford-on-Avon Railway weighbridge office and part of the goods shed. This weighbridge was replaced in the late 1930s during station alterations and became an office for the goods yard. Notice the very rudimentary buffer stop.
R. S. CARPENTER

This view from the up platform, facing Stratford in 1934, shows the station buildings, East Junction Box, signals and goods yard, etc. Two of Messrs. Stevco wagons can again be seen in the distance on the coal siding. They were a local concern and could be found at a number of yards in the Birmingham–Leamington–Stratford areas during the 1920s-30s. C. L. MOWAT

Something of this nature had clearly taken place at Bearley, although the station was not itself a country lorry centre. More importantly, there was also an upsurge in roadstone and other mineral traffic during the later 1930s, and this type of bulk freight traffic amounted to 6,569 tons in 1936, 15,730 tons in 1937 and 14,353 tons in 1938.

Domestic coal traffic was another form of inwards freight traffic, and in most years Bearley handled about 2,300 tons per annum. The coal was supplied by Warwickshire pits and distributed by locally-based coal merchants such as Mr Snell, who operated from Bearley goods yard. At this period, coal came from the pits of Baddesley, Newdigate and Coventry collieries.

Other inwards traffic included animal feed, fertilizers and variable amounts of general merchandise. Throughout most of the 1930s, Bearley dealt with little more than 300 tons of general goods traffic per annum, but in 1938 this meagre figure increased to 1,052 tons, possibly because of the growth of carted 'smalls' traffic that had hitherto been handled at other stations.

Bearley's staffing establishment rose from seven in 1903 to eleven by 1913, following the opening of the North Warwickshire line and a consequent need for extra signalmen at Bearley North and Bearley West junctions. In 1925 the station provided employment for sixteen people including one Class 5 station master, four porters, eight signalmen, one gatekeeper (at Edstone Level Crossing), one part-time cleaning woman and one general clerk.

This same basic establishment remained without major alteration for several years, and by the 1930s, the staff included one Class 5 station master, two leading porters, two porters, eight signalmen, one general clerk and one gatekeeper.

There were no lorry drivers at Bearley itself, collection and delivery arrangements in the area being concentrated on the nearby 'country lorry centre' at Stratford-upon-Avon. It appears that local collections and deliveries were handled by a vehicle from Stratford that was sent out to Bearley station on a daily basis, the drivers involved being based at Stratford rather than Bearley.

Bearley's station masters included John Twist, who was in charge of the station during the 1870s, and William Morewood, who remained at the station for over twenty years between the early 1880s and about 1905. By 1908, the station master was Charles Overbury, but he left in 1909, and was replaced by Joseph Billington, who came to Bearley after previous service at Cropredy, on the Oxford to Birmingham main line. Mr Billington was still at Bearley in 1916, though he had gone by the early 1920s, by which time the local station master was Joseph Tolley.

In 1938 the GWR embarked on a scheme to widen the Hatton–Bearley section to take double track. By this time, this route was becoming heavily used by freight trains bound for South Wales, chiefly iron ore workings from the Banbury area. It was also used for excursion traffic during the summer timetables, as well as a diversionary route to the North Warwicks line for through passenger and freight workings to the west and South Wales.

Work on the widening commenced in May 1938 and at Bearley station this entailed the rebuilding of the waiting room on the down platform and the addition of a footbridge linking the platforms. The new works were brought into use from 2nd July 1939. Finally, during the early part of the war, two new sidings were laid in on the down side for the delivery of materials for a nearby RAF establishment. After the war, these sidings were used to store wagons awaiting repairs.

ALONG THE ROUTE

Alcester branch trains departed from the down platform at Bearley station and diverged north-westwards from the Hatton–Stratford line alongside Bearley East Junction signal box, curving sharply to the right by means of a double junction. Immediately beyond, the line became single and, on a slight falling gradient, entered a shallow cutting, followed by a straight stretch through open farmland, and through a further cutting as it approached Bearley North Junction. Here the branch merged with the North Warwickshire line (opened in 1907–8) for about 150 yards before diverging

Note: Post-1908 Engineering Department distances from Bearley North Junction are used throughout this route description.

Bearley East Junction Signal Box was a brick-and-timber design with a gable roof and small-paned windows, such boxes being typical of GWR architectural practice during the late Victorian period. It became the East Junction Box in 1907 when the nearby North Warwicks line opened, creating a triangle at Bearley, and the former section of the Alcester branch between the East Junction and the North Junction became known as the North Curve. The wagons behind the box in this 1956 photo were standing on the two sidings laid down during the war for the Air Ministry. After the war, they were used for stabling crippled and stored wagons. P. J. GARLAND

The single-line section from Hatton West Junction to Bearley East Junction was doubled on 2nd July 1939. The section from Bearley East Junction to West Junction had been doubled in 1907 in conjunction with the North Warwicks opening. This view, taken c.1939 just before the double-line operations came into force, shows the fireman of a '31XX' 2-6-2 tank on a Leamington–Stratford local surrendering the single-line staff as the train was pulling away from the station. A. T. LOCKE
CTY. KIDDERMINSTER RAILWAY MUSEUM

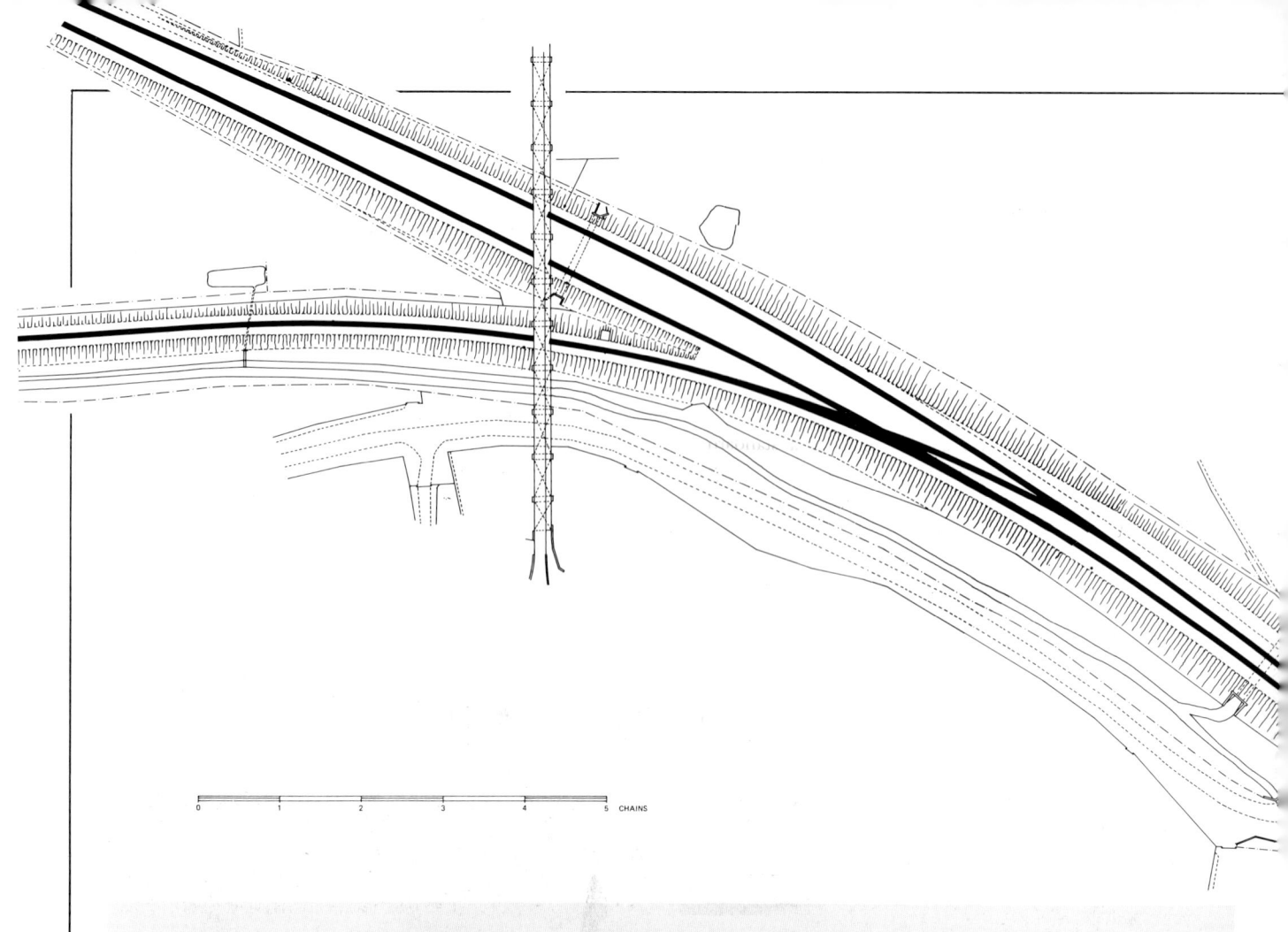

Taken from the North Junction Signal Box during the summer of 1947, this picture shows Bearley North Junction with the North Curve (original Alcester branch) diverging to the left towards East Junction, and the North Warwicks line curving to the right to join the West Junction.
P. J. GARLAND

again in a westerly direction. The new line, superimposed on the original Alcester route, had the effect of breaking the Alcester line into two block sections, the first, from Bearley East Junction to Bearley North Junction, being worked by electric tablet. Alcester Branch Junction was situated on a low embankment that swept through a shallow valley in a great curve. The surroundings here were entirely pastoral, the landscape being characterised by open farmland interspersed with trees and hedgerows.

Bearley North Junction was controlled from a standard GWR signal cabin on the east side of the line, which seems to have opened around December 1906 in connection with the construction of the North Warwickshire line. The box, which was just 45 chains from Bearley, was a timber-framed structure clad in horizontal weatherboarding. It had a hipped roof, and its operating floor was glazed with distinctive five-pane windows, which were supposed to give signalmen an unimpeded view of the line; such boxes were widely used throughout the GWR system from about 1900 onwards (though most examples were of brick-and-timber construction).

In operational terms, Bearley North Junction signal box was significant in that it marked the end of the single-line section from Bearley East Junction, and the commencement of the 6 miles 6 chains section between Bearley North

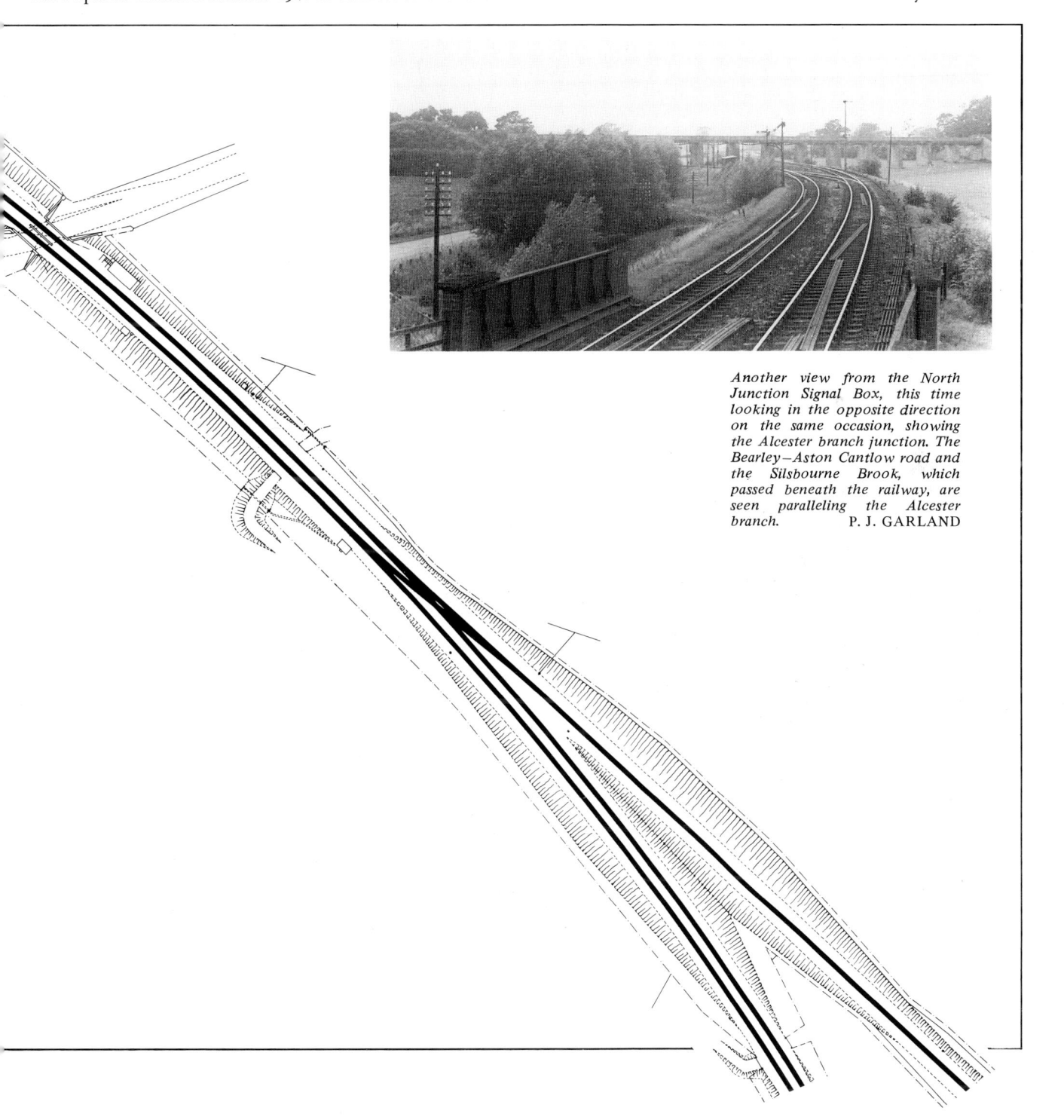

Another view from the North Junction Signal Box, this time looking in the opposite direction on the same occasion, showing the Alcester branch junction. The Bearley–Aston Cantlow road and the Silsbourne Brook, which passed beneath the railway, are seen paralleling the Alcester branch. P. J. GARLAND

A panoramic view of the junctions as seen from the towpath on the aqueduct on 12th June 1934, featuring the down home junction bracket signal with repeaters on the left and Bearley North Junction Signal Box. The Silsbourne Brook lined with willows and the Bearley–Aston Cantlow road feature again in the centre of the picture. The branch junction stop signal and PW hut also feature on the right.
C. L. MOWAT

'517' class 0-4-2T No. 1425 with an Alcester-bound auto, approaching the aqueduct on 30th May 1934.
P. W. ROBINSON

Junction and Alcester; here, the single-line tablets were exchanged, and branch trains were then able to enter their own line for the main part of the journey to Alcester.

Having left the main line, Alcester trains passed beneath the Stratford-on-Avon Canal, which was carried across the valley at this point on the Edstone Aqueduct. This impressive engineering feature consisted of fourteen spans, the waterway being carried in a series of cast-iron 'troughs', which were supported on slightly tapered brick piers. The aqueduct had been designed and built by William James (1771–1837), the well-known canal and tramway promoter. It was opened for navigation on 24th June 1816, when the Stratford-on-Avon Canal was opened throughout to Stratford, and was one of the largest cast-iron structures of its type in the country, its total length being 475ft; its maximum height above local ground level was 28ft. (It was probably named after the nearby Edstone Park Estate.)

This historic aqueduct crossed over both the North Warwickshire route and the Alcester branch, the up and down North Warwickshire lines passing between the seventh and eighth spans (from the north end) while the branch ran through the tenth span.

It was from this aqueduct that the Alcester branch engine took water at frequent intervals during the day, running

THE LINE DESCRIBED

The aqueduct as seen from the Bearley–Aston Cantlow road on 12th June 1934. C. L. MOWAT

A closer view of the wooden-cased delivery pipe and water column arrangement mounted on the ivy-clad brick pier of the aqueduct, with the fire-devil below it, on 6th June 1953. The branch stop signal was mounted on a concrete post which dated from the re-opening of the branch in December 1922. The wooden-posted signal in the foreground probably dated from the 1907 alterations, whilst the 3½ milepost on the extreme left was erected by BR(W) in March 1951 when the line to Great Alne was used for wagon storage. The route mileage was altered accordingly.
P. J. GARLAND

light-engine down from Bearley station before setting out with the branch train for Alcester. Water was drawn from the canal by means of a lagged pipe in a vertical wooden box, terminating in a wheeled valve and elbow, from which hung the conventional leather 'bag' through which water was fed to the locomotive. A ladder enabled the engine crews to reach the operating wheel and there was one of the customary fire devils placed beneath the pipe and the leather delivery bag to help safeguard against frost.

A form of filter was originally fitted to the top or head end of the pipe to prevent leaves, twigs and other floating debris from entering locomotive tanks, though local legend asserted that by the 1930s this had in fact rusted away, thereby allowing fish to enter the tanks, the branch '48XX' supposedly carrying the sign 'Frying tonight' for obvious reasons!

Before leaving the canal, it should perhaps be mentioned that this railway-owned waterway fell into disuse below Lapworth after World War One, and one of the last boats to use the southern section of the canal had to be partially unloaded in order for it to reach its destination. A maintenance boat forced its way through to Stratford in 1947, but the route then became impassable until the waterway was restored for navigation by volunteers in the early 1960s.

Beyond the aqueduct, the branch paralleled the North Warwicks line for about a quarter of a mile, in company with the Silsbourne Brook and the Bearley–Aston Cantlow road on the left, to a farm occupation crossing known as

The Bearley North Junction outer home signal was situated some 10 chains west of the aqueduct, as seen in this view facing Bearley on 6th June 1953. Its concrete post again dated from the branch re-opening in December 1922. The telephone mounted on the base of the post provided communication with the signalman. The Silsbourne Brook was situated immediately behind the screen of willow trees on the left, and the underbridge just apparent in the distance carried the branch over the brook. Neals Crossing, referred to in the text, was beyond whilst a fixed distant signal for the junction was located some 10 chains or so away, behind the photographer. P. J. GARLAND

Neales Crossing, where the brook passed beneath the branch by means of a steel-span bridge at 0 miles 24½ chains. With the stream now flowing beside the line on the right-hand side, and with the Bearley to Aston Cantlow road veering off in a southerly direction, down trains continued through pleasant agricultural land for about one mile. Curving gradually south-westwards, the railway then entered a shallow cutting for a short distance and then passed beneath a road overbridge at 1 miles 34¼ chains. The bridge was constructed of stone and cast iron, its abutments, wing walls and parapets being of local Wilmcote grey stonework laid in snecked or interrupted courses, while the main transverse girders were made of iron.

Aston Cantlow Halt, the first stopping place, was only a short distance further on at 1 mile 37 chains. It was opened on 18th December 1922 after the inhabitants of the surrounding

The view towards Bearley from the road overbridge (seen below) in 1949. J. H. MOSS

The road overbridge at 1 mile 34¼ chains viewed from the halt on 28th February 1953. J. H. MOSS

Aston Cantlow Halt, as seen from the roadbridge, overshadowed by adjoining elm trees on a summer's day during the late 1930s. The road leading to the village of Aston Cantlow, about half a mile distant, is seen on the left. Note the land behind in use as a vegetable patch.

LENS OF SUTTON

THE LINE DESCRIBED

area had petitioned the GWR for a new station to serve the needs of people living in Aston Cantlow and Little Alne. The halt consisted of a 200ft, sleeper-built platform on the down side of the running line and an arc-roofed corrugated-iron waiting shed. Public access was by means of a sloping pathway from the adjacent Bearley to Aston Cantlow Road.

The platform was fenced with post-and-rail fencing, and at night the halt was lit by oil lamps in GWR-style tapered glass lanterns. A corrugated-iron lamp hut was also provided at the foot of the Bearley end of the platform to house oil and other ancillary items to trim the lamps, etc.

For administrative purposes, Aston Cantlow Halt came under the control of the Great Alne station master, and its traffic returns were included with those from Great Alne.

At this point the railway drew close to the River Alne, which lay some 150 yards or so on the opposite side of the line to the halt, whilst elm trees grew near the T-junction of the roads near the road overbridge, flanking the verges of the lane up to Little Alne and the land adjacent to the railway boundary fence in front of the halt. From here the railway continued south-westwards through low-lying meadowland that tended to suffer from flooding during periods of wet

ASTON CANTLOW HALT

The halt, facing Bearley c.1930, showing the road overbridge and the pathway from the nearby road. The corrugated iron hut situated at the far end of the platform served as a lamp hut.
COLLECTION JOHN PLATT

Collett 0–4–2T No. 4801 approaching Aston Cantlow Halt with a Bearley-bound branch auto during 1935. MAURICE DEANE

weather. Just before reaching the river, a cattle creep passed beneath the line, then the river was crossed at 2 miles 13¾ chains by means of a 43ft 3in girder span supported by brick piers with three brick-built flood arches at the Bearley end. This structure was severely damaged by flooding in January 1901 when the Rivers Alne and Arrow burst their banks. The main bridge girders were washed away and deposited in the river alongside the abutments, whilst the brickwork in the flood arches was badly cracked. The bridge was rebuilt with new girders and to this day the original ones lie in the bed of the river where they fell. Afterwards, in view of the

A June 1993 snapshot of the decaying remains of the River Alne bridge at 2 miles 13¾ chains.
R. S. CARPENTER

cracks that weakened the structure, motive power permitted over the branch was restricted, and frequent inspections were carried out by a diver who was periodically sent from Plymouth. On these occasions the local permanent way men were required to pump air to him while he operated in about sixteen feet of water. The structure underwent further extensive repairs in 1926 when the bridge was redecked with 9in timbers and additional stiffeners, gussets, etc, to the main girders.

Beyond the river bridge the line was carried over the Aston Brook by means of a twin-span girder bridge at 2 miles 15¼ chains and, with the River Alne now flowing on the south side of the line, trains wound through lush meadowland. At 2 miles 53 chains the branch passed beneath another road overbridge which, like its counterpart at Aston Cantlow, was of stone and girder construction; this bridge carried a minor lane across the line.

Looking along the line towards Bearley near the 2½ milepost c.1950. The Aston Cantlow Mill was situated just 'off camera' in the distance to the right. Notice the PW hut in the distance.
COLLECTION R. S. CARPENTER

The bridge at 2 miles 53 chains. This picture was also taken facing Bearley.
AUTHORS' COLLECTION

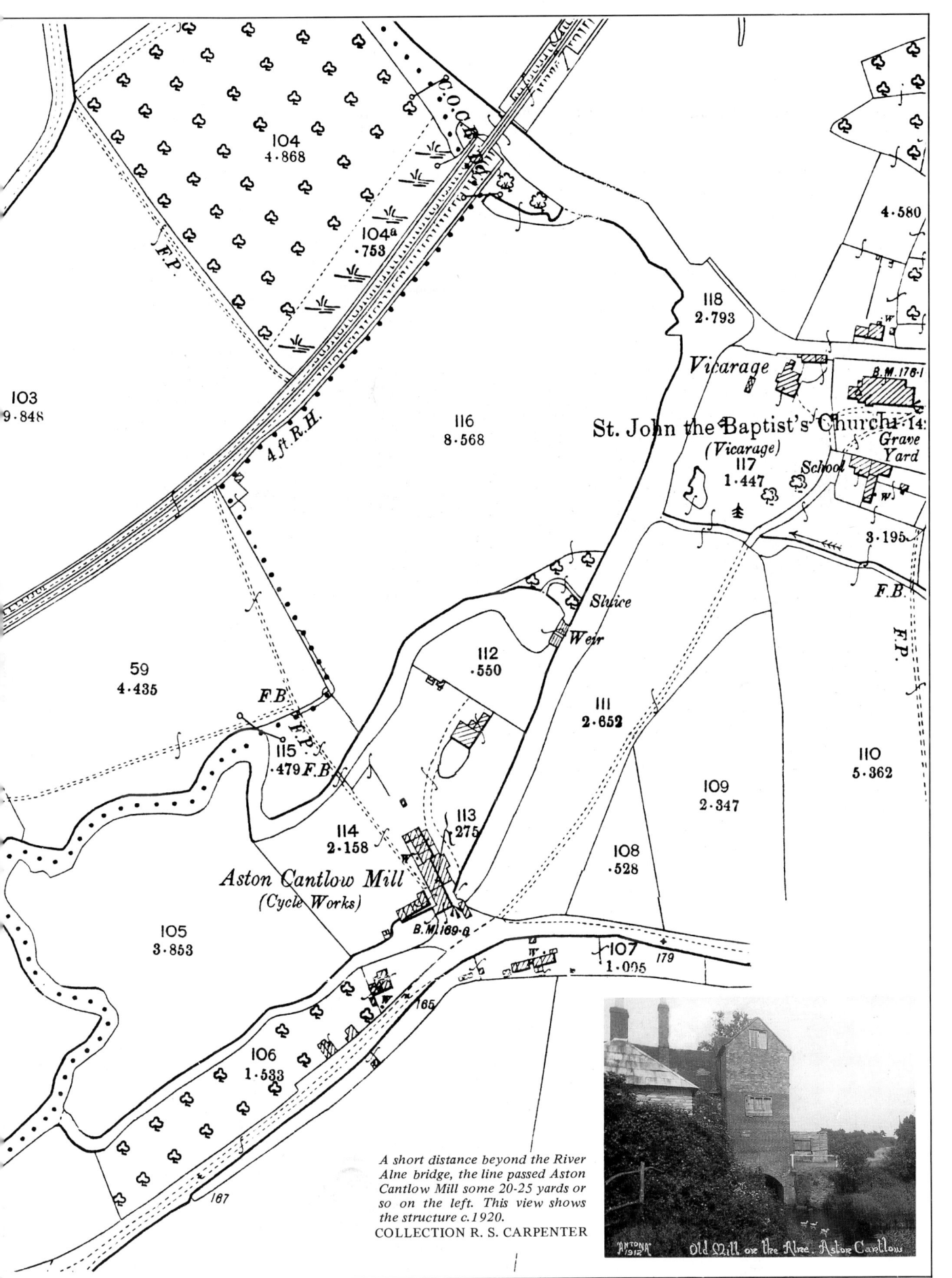

A short distance beyond the River Alne bridge, the line passed Aston Cantlow Mill some 20-25 yards or so on the left. This view shows the structure c.1920.
COLLECTION R. S. CARPENTER

Taken from 25-inch Ordnance Survey for 1905. (Crown copyright reserved)

Yet another view along the line, facing Bearley c.1950. The road overbridge is in fact obscured by the 'Whistle' sign. These pictures convey some idea of the landscape in this vicinity, with elm and oak trees dominating the skyline, and hedgerows and post-and-wire fencing bordering the company's property. The River Alne kept fairly close company with the line, especially in the vicinity of this photograph, where its course is marked by the cluster of elm and willow trees.
AUTHOR'S COLLECTION

THE LINE DESCRIBED

The railway was, for most of its length, fenced with typical GWR post-and-wire fencing, though in practice the boundaries of railway property on each side of the line were partly delineated by luxuriant hedgerows, which had presumably encroached upon the original fencing (though some Victorian railways were fenced with quickset hedges from their inception). Edward Booker, who worked on the Alcester branch as a ganger in the 1930s, recalled that his duties included mowing both sides of the line with a scythe throughout its distance from Bearley to Alcester, together with hedge trimming as 'most of the fences were hedges'.

Mr Booker also remembered that there were many willow trees alongside the branch, particularly at the Bearley end, where they were thickly planted along the Silsbourne Brook. These trees were regularly pollarded, the long thin sticks so produced being sold to potters in the Stoke-on-Trent area who used them to weave baskets in which to carry their products.

Curving onto a westerly alignment, the railway reached Spencer's Crossing, by means of which a private road to the nearby Great Alne Corn Mill crossed the branch. The gated crossing was protected by working distant signals, and a small brick-built cottage was provided on the up side of the line for the resident gatekeeper.

From around 1922–23, when the branch re-opened, the family occupying the crossing cottage were the Jeffs: Tommy, who was employed as a ganger on the branch at that time, his wife Kate, who worked the level crossing, and their son Frederick.

Edward Booker recalls:

'When I worked down the branch, the cottage at Spencer's Crossing was occupied by retired ganger Tommy Jeffs and his wife. Tommy died during the mid-1930s and his widow continued working the level crossing for some years afterwards. The gates were opened and closed by hand, their normal position being opened to the road. The small ground frame had levers for the up and down distant signals, and a locking lever

General view of Spencer, Son & Hancox Mill c.1930 with the archway for the River Alne alongside.
THE OLD GREAT ALNE VILLAGE BOOK COLLECTION

for the gates. It was situated between the crossing cottage and the railway, giving a good view in both the up and down directions. Above the ground frame was a 'Train on Line' indicator instrument, and, I think, also a telephone.'

Mrs Jeffs moved from the crossing cottage to live in Great Alne in 1939, probably when the branch closed that September. Her place was taken by Mr & Mrs Mortimer, who stayed there until 1942, and they were followed by Mr

The former crossing keeper's cottage at Spencer's Crossing seen shortly before demolition in 1965. The porch protected the entrance whilst the lean-to part of the building on the right housed the scullery and kitchen. The building was constructed in red brick with a slate roof, and dated from the opening of the line in 1876. This picture was taken from the trackbed facing Great Alne.
THE OLD GREAT ALNE VILLAGE BOOK COLLECTION

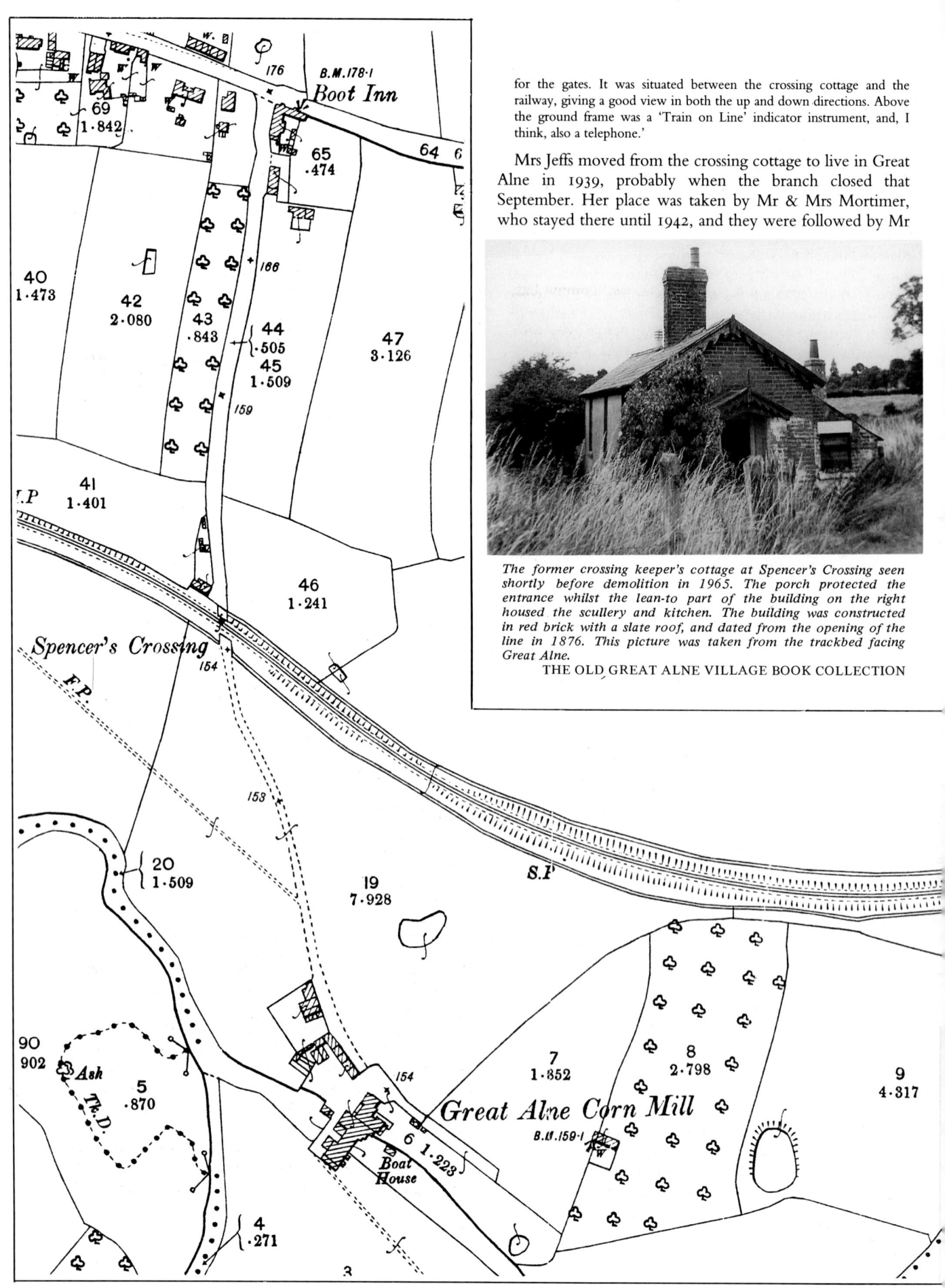

Taken from 25-inch Ordnance Survey for 1905. (Crown copyright reserved)

THE LINE DESCRIBED

& Mrs Fletcher and their three children, who stayed there until 1954. Mr Fletcher worked in the nearby Spencer's Mill whilst Mrs Fletcher worked the level crossing for the then meagre traffic from Bearley to Great Alne, which, by that time, was confined to the Maudsley works trains and the twice-weekly freight train.

The next occupants were the Davis family, who remained there until the late 1950s, when the cottage was abandoned and the line was used for wagon storage.

Mrs Diane Wright, whose great uncle was Tommy Jeffs, and Mrs Betty Morrison (formally Davis) recalled the cramped conditions of the crossing cottage, which dated from the opening of the line in 1876. There were three small rooms, and a lean-to scullery with a corrugated-iron extension which contained a hand pump to raise water from a well. By the mid-1950s the well had dried up and water had to be obtained from a pump at the top of Mill lane. Lighting in the cottage was by paraffin lamps.

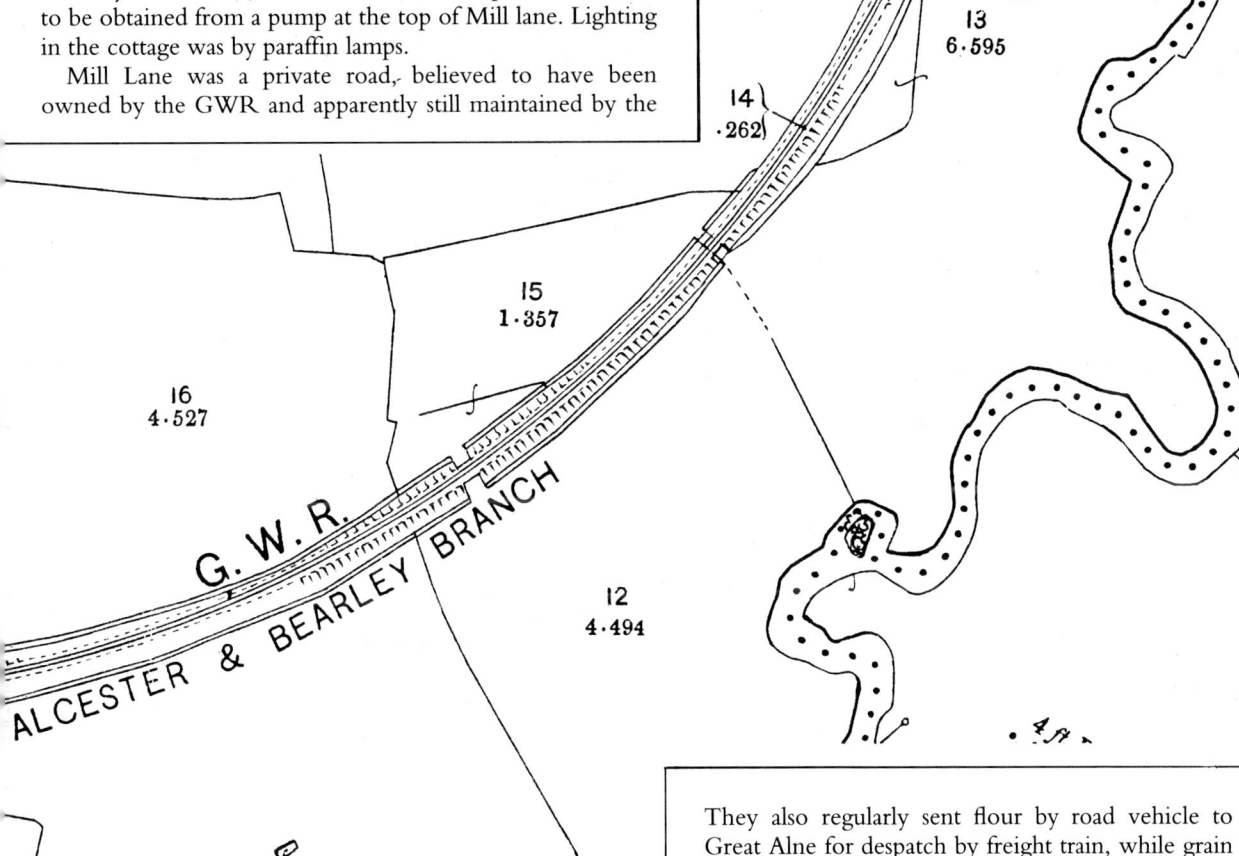

Mill Lane was a private road, believed to have been owned by the GWR and apparently still maintained by the railway in 2004. For legal reasons, the road was closed once a year; Betty Morrison recalled the placing of a chain across the top end of Mill lane around Easter time.

Great Alne Mill, which was situated on the south side of the railway, was a water-powered corn mill on the banks of the Alne. Like most other mills, it occupied a very old site, the first reference to a mill in the vicinity being in 1804. For many years it was operated by Spencer Son & Hancox who, in the early 1930s, supplied many local bakeries with flour. They also regularly sent flour by road vehicle to nearby Great Alne for despatch by freight train, while grain formed an important source of incoming traffic.

In common with many other isolated level crossings in rural areas, Spencer's Crossing was worked as simply as possible, the instrument provided being linked to the boxes at Bearley North Junction and Alcester, so that the gatekeeper was given a visual and audible warning when trains entered the single-line section.

From Spencer's Crossing the line turned south-westwards as it neared the intermediate station at Great Alne at 3 miles 58¼ chains, some 4 miles 29 chains from the start of the journey at Bearley.

GREAT ALNE

This view looking east towards Bearley was taken from the eastern end of Great Alne goods yard c.1950. The concrete-post up distant for Spencer's Crossing features in the centre whilst Spencer's Crossing Cottage is just visible in the distance. One of the gangers' huts features on the left whilst the small hut on the right covered a two-lever ground frame controlling the adjacent pointwork.
COLLECTION R. S. CARPENTER

The station was situated close to the banks of the River Alne with the road from Alcester to Wootton-Wawen immediately behind the station, flanked by a row of elms. The lane from Haselor village approached the station from the south and crossed the line at the Alcester end of the platform by means of a level crossing with hand-operated gates.

Great Alne, like its neighbouring village of Aston Cantlow, was a largely self-contained farming community. The station was provided with a substantial red-brick two-storey combined station house and offices to William Clarke's design. It had a platform canopy, a roof of grey slate, and red-brick ornamental chimney stacks. The 230ft single curved platform was faced with red brick and paved with diamond-pattern bricks.

The goods yard was originally provided with a single siding about 300ft in length for 14 wagons or so, trailing from the Alcester direction. In January 1908 the siding was converted to a loop siding with an additional two-lever ground frame at the Bearley end of the loop, and a standard GW corrugated-iron goods lock-up was erected on the platform around this time. The office for the yard weighbridge, situated immediately behind the platform fence, was a small red-brick structure dating from the opening of the station. When the rails were temporarily removed in 1917, the goods lock-up also disappeared, presumably for re-use elsewhere, but when the station was reopened in 1922, a similar structure was erected on the same site and, incidentally, the yard trackwork was relaid to the pre-1917 layout with the addition of a long mileage siding along the rear boundary of the goods yard area.

Generally, it was the practice for mixed trains from Bearley to Alcester to use the siding connection trailing from

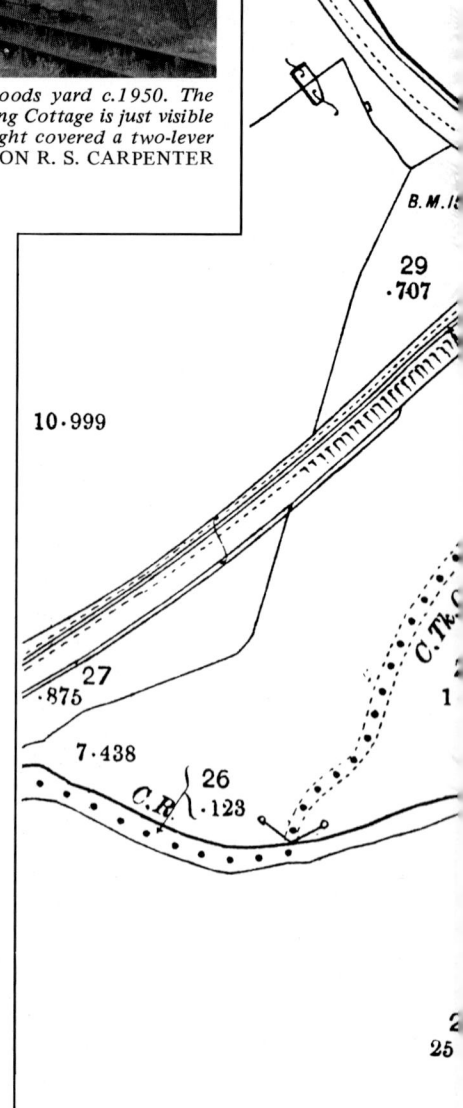

Taken from 25-inch Ordnance Survey for 1905. (Crown copyright reserved)

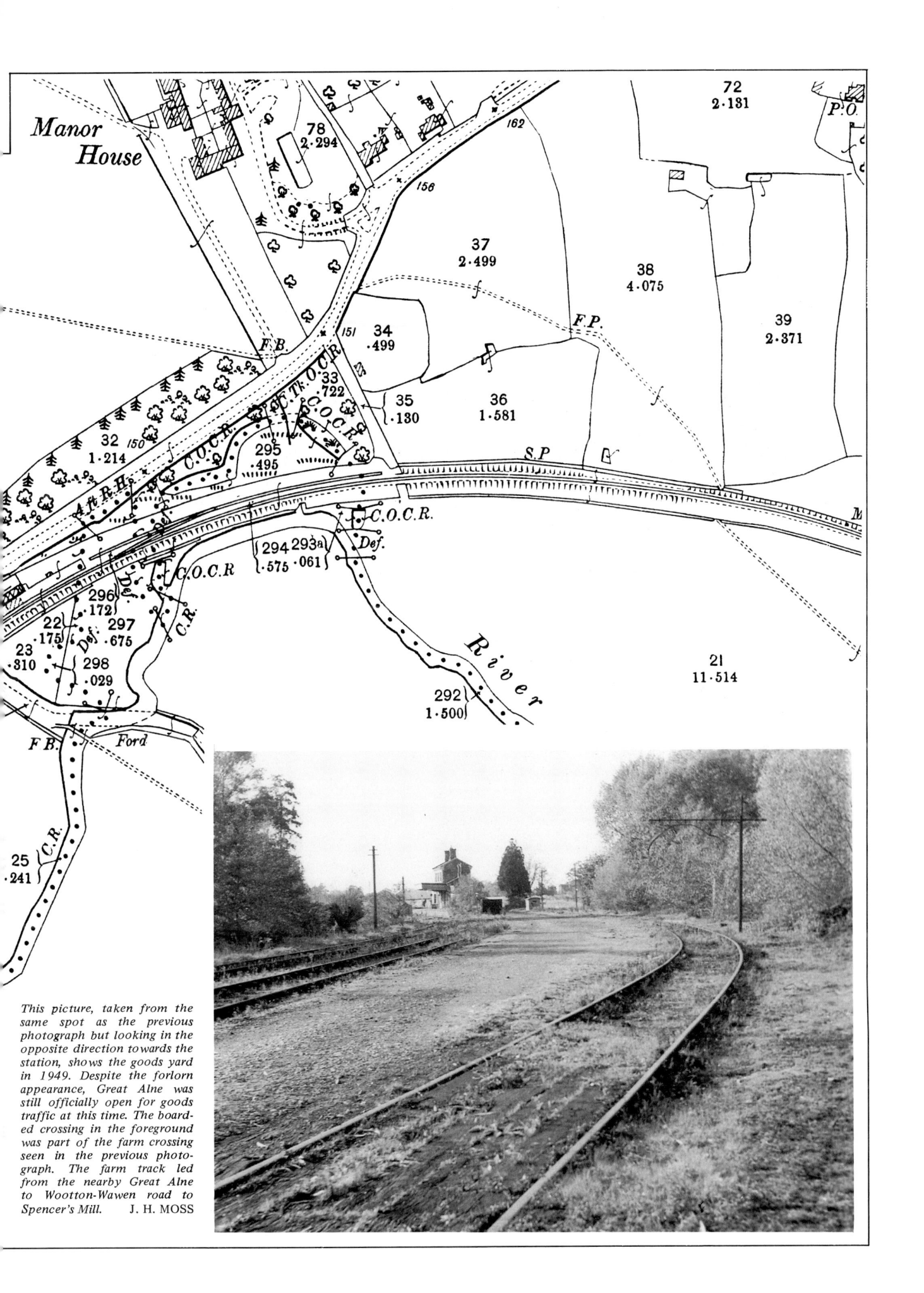

This picture, taken from the same spot as the previous photograph but looking in the opposite direction towards the station, shows the goods yard in 1949. Despite the forlorn appearance, Great Alne was still officially open for goods traffic at this time. The boarded crossing in the foreground was part of the farm crossing seen in the previous photograph. The farm track led from the nearby Great Alne to Wootton-Wawen road to Spencer's Mill. J. H. MOSS

A further 1949 view of the goods yard taken from the end of the station platform, looking east towards Bearley.　　　J. H. MOSS

STAFF AND TRAFFIC AT GREAT ALNE

It is believed that the first station master at Great Alne was Joseph Shaw, who is mentioned in the 1876 edition of *Kelly's Directory of Warwickshire*, By 1884, however, Mr Shaw had been replaced by Joseph Barber, who by 1892 had himself been replaced by Frederick Jones as 'Station Master and Goods Agent' at Great Alne.

At the turn of the century, the station was being supervised by John Taylor, and *Kelly's Directory* reveals that he was in office in 1908 but had gone by 1912, his successor being Thomas Stacey.

In 1916 the station master was Charles Boucher, while in 1924 the local station master was J. Andrews. Another station master recalled by former railway staff was Mr Gardner, who is said to have been in charge of the station during the 1920s, though by the 1930s he had been replaced by Mr Tombs. At that time, the station had a staff of four, comprising one Class 5 station master, two porters and the female gate-keeper at nearby Spencer's Crossing.

In 1932 Great Alne was placed under the control of the Bearley station master, and thereafter it was manned by just one Grade 1 porter, though local residents seem to have referred to him as 'the station master' even though this was not his actual grade.

In general, Great Alne issued about 5,000 tickets per annum during the early and mid-twentieth century. In 1903, for example, there were 5,204 ticket sales, while in 1923 the station dealt with 4,503 passenger bookings. In 1934, 2,763 tickets were issued, together with 53 season tickets.

Great Alne was less important than Bearley in terms of goods traffic, typical figures being 4,230 tons in 1923 and 2,774 tons in 1931. By the late 1930s, the station was dealing with little more than 1,700 tons of goods traffic per annum, much of this being grain, timber and general merchandise. By that time, a considerable amount of traffic was being lost to road transport, and the branch was clearly entering a period of decline.

The late Maurice Long, a lifelong railwayman, started his railway career at the station in 1923 as lad porter and stayed there until 1928 when he transferred to the S&T Department. He recalls that the staff in 1923 were station master Mr Gardner, who was also responsible for Aston Cantlow Halt, a clerk, a lad porter, and an adult porter.

The porter's duties included going round the surrounding district at the end of each month collecting outstanding 'bills' owed to the railway, working the level-crossing gates adjacent to the station platform, maintenance of the station and platform lamps, level-crossing gate lamps, and the lamp on the up fixed distant signal (along the line in the Alcester direction) protecting the approach to Great Alne station crossing. The porters also had to pump water from a well situated behind the gents' toilet for the station's entire water supply and each day a porter was dispatched to fill and trim the oil lamps at the halt at Aston Cantlow.

Parcels were regularly dispatched and received but although Great Alne was not equipped with a cattle dock, sheep and crates of small pigs (whitebacks) were occasionally unloaded onto the passenger platform.

During the 1920s the goods yard was often full of wagons. Incoming goods traffic included grain in sheeted opens from Avonmouth Docks for Spencer Son & Hancox of Great Alne Mill, the quantities varying from week to week – 'sometimes 1–2 wagons, other times 3–4'. On arrival, a labourer, was sent down from the mill with a sack truck to unload the wagons. 'If they had peephole doors', Maurice assisted with the unloading. Other incoming traffic included cattlecake and animal feedstuffs for local farmers and supplies of domestic coal.

A large storage tank was provided about 1924 for Fosters of Studley for storage of paraffin. The tank, said to have been an old boiler, was set into the bank behind the back siding. The paraffin arrived in cans and was manually discharged into the tank.

Outgoing traffic included milk, which was dispatched by the first train of the day for Bearley. The churns were generally loaded into the goods brake van but sometimes the auto-coach had to be used as well if there were too many to load into the brake van. Frequently a porter travelled from Great Alne up to Bearley to assist the guard with unloading the churns, which were generally destined for Birmingham.

On occasions, rounds of locally-felled timber were dispatched from Great Alne. This was brought to the station by Masons, a local haulage firm from Aston Cantlow, and was loaded on to bolster wagons by means of a portable crane which came from Hartlebury. Some hay and straw was sent out from the station, as was flour from Spencer's Mill, and willow poles, which were used for making hurdles, fencing, etc.

There was also another mill on the banks of the Alne, close to the railway, near Aston Cantlow, which during the 1920s manufactured brushes amongst other products. This mill was owned by the Row family, who also had interests in horticulture, and the rearing of white-back pigs. The mill provided some business for the railway via Great Alne station.

This 1949 view shows the western end of the goods yard, the entrance to which was on the far right by the buffer stop of the back siding, and the corrugated-iron lamp hut. The black square structure alongside the siding loop points was a sleeper-built store for the station coal. Unfortunately, in this photo the coal store obscures the weigh bridge, which was situated behind the rear of the passenger platform. The single pitch roof of the weigh office just features in the photo on page 23 but there are no other photos of it. The weighing machine was renewed in 1931 when it was replaced by a 20-ton machine with a 16ft x 8ft plate. Authority for this new work was given on 22nd January 1931, when the GWR Traffic Committee agreed that an existing secondhand machine (No. 4570) would be transferred to Great Alne from Birmingham Moor Street at an estimated cost of £210. The hut to the left of the siding points covered a 5-lever ground frame for the Great Alne up and down distant signals, the siding loop points and gate bolt for the level crossing, whilst the black-painted hut contained a lineside telephone alongside. J. H. MOSS

The forecourt elevation of Great Alne station in May 1953, two years after official closure to freight traffic. The doorway gave access to the station house, and public access to the station was from the platform side via the ramp and wicket gate on the right. By this date the station house had been let out for private occupation and by 1957/58 the former booking office/waiting room was adapted for use as a shop which became the Great Alne Post Office and village store. One of the authors remembers visiting it to purchase ice cream with his parents during the late 1950s. The Great Alne to Wootton-Wawen road features in the foreground. W. A. CAMWELL

THE ALCESTER BRANCH

An Edwardian postcard view of Great Alne station, postmarked 'Alcester November 27th 1905'. The tall trees behind the station flanked the Alcester–Wootton Wawen road and formed a striking feature of the station when viewed from either the field opposite or the lane to Haselor.
COLLECTION GRAHAM MORRIS

Another of the Joe Moss photographs taken in 1949 from alongside the siding ground frame. The single-storey booking office portion at this end of the station building contained two rooms, the ladies' waiting room being at the eastern extremity of the building whilst the general waiting room was to the left of the ladies' room (when viewed from the front, or platform elevation). The ladies' room and the general waiting room were both provided with external doors from the platform, and there was, in addition, an internal door in the intervening wall. The gentlemen's lavatory and urinal was situated in a small, rectangular extension beyond the ladies' room, and this extension also contained the ladies' lavatory, access to which was via a connecting door from the main block. The booking office was situated to the west of the waiting room within the two-storey 'house' portion, and this arrangement ensured that the station safe and other sensitive items were placed in the most secure part of the building. The booking office, waiting room and ladies' room were all protected by the platform canopy, which was supported on cast-iron brackets bearing the initials 'AR' (i.e. Alcester Railway) in their decorative spandrels. The canopy was edged with deeply-cut tongue-and-groove fretwork, as already explained this same design being employed on other Clarke buildings throughout the GWR system. The building was constructed of English bond brickwork, in which each row of headers (bricks laid laterally) was alternated with a course of stretchers (bricks laid longitudinally). The window and door apertures were square-headed with stone lintels, while the windows were of the large-paned sliding sash type; there was, in addition, a projecting bay window towards the west end of the station master's house, and this contributed a further element of visual interest to the platform frontage. The roofs were gabled, with stone copings on the top of each gable, and decorative features known as 'kneelers' at the bottom of each parapet. There were four chimney stacks, all of which were of typical William Clarke design.
J. H. MOSS

THE LINE DESCRIBED

the platform end of the loop, whilst trains from Alcester used the connection trailing from the Bearley end. The mileage siding would have been shunted by Bearley-bound trains, although it seems that by the mid-1930s the back road or mileage siding was seldom used.

The ground frames controlling access to the yard were unlocked using the single-line tablet. Like Spencer's Crossing, there were two distant signals protecting Great Alne station level crossing; the up distant was situated 500 yards from the Alcester side of the crossing whilst the down distant was located between Spencer's Crossing and the Spencer's Crossing up distant signal. These signals and the gate bolt for the level crossing gates were operated from a ground frame adjacent to the platform. A lineside telephone hut was also provided alongside whilst the 'Train-on-Line' indicator instruments were located in the booking office.

The level crossing over the Great Alne–Haselor road in 1949, showing the grass-carpeted track of the then disused section of the branch curving away towards Alcester. The crossing was protected by two distant signals, the down signal being positioned 469 yards to the east of the crossing.
J. H. MOSS

The last of the 1949 views of Great Alne station shows the scotch-block placed across the track denoting limit of operations of the branch from Bearley.
J. H. MOSS

The branch auto-train of the late 1930s era, headed by an unidentified 48XX Collett tank with what is believed to have been auto-trailer No. 83, approaching the level crossing at Great Alne station. This picture was taken from the Great Alne–Haselor road and features in the background the council houses built alongside the Great Alne–Alcester road.
COLLECTION
R. S. CARPENTER

This view, looking along the branch towards Alcester from the level crossing at Great Alne, is believed to have been taken in the summer of 1939. The signal wire alongside the track on the left controlled the Great Alne up distant signal situated round the bend some 500 yards away.
A. T. LOCKE
CTY. KIDDERMINSTER
RAILWAY MUSEUM

THE LINE DESCRIBED

The skew girder bridge near Kinwarton, seen here in 1960 looking towards Alcester along the B4089 Alcester–Wootton-Wawen road shortly before the lifting of the line between Alcester and Great Alne and the removal of the bridge girders. RICHARD KING CTY. WARWICKSHIRE RECORD OFFICE (PH417-31)

Leaving Great Alne, the line headed due west on a dead straight course for Alcester. Parting company with the River Alne, trains were faced with a slight ascent as they approached the Great Alne to Alcester Road on a low embankment. At 4 miles 38¾ chains the railway was carried across the road on a skew girder bridge that was supported on red and blue brick abutments.

After gradually climbing on gradients of 1 in 80 and 1 in 146, the summit was reached at Captain's Hill, close to the hamlet of Kinwarton, where a surprisingly deep cutting was spanned by a three-arch red and blue brick bridge, which at 4 miles 69¼ chains carried a minor cart track over the line. Beyond the bridge, and continuing on its straight course, the line descended on a 1 in 66 gradient, followed by a stretch at 1 in 275 and 1 in 750 for nearly half a mile down to the MR junction. This climb was known as Gerrards Bank by the GW loco crews. The climb up to Captain's Hill from both directions was the steepest section of the line and mixed trains sometimes made heavy weather of climbing up from Alcester.

For the final stretch down to the MR junction at Alcester, the line was carried mostly on an embankment across open farmland, passing over a farm track by means of a single-arch underbridge constructed in red brick at 5 miles 9 chains, followed shortly afterwards by an occupation crossing where a track led to a nearby farm. Shortly afterwards, yet another red-brick single-arch bridge at 5 miles 53¼ chains crossed yet another farm track as the line approached the water meadows and where willow trees marked the course of the River Arrow.

An MR-pattern (working) distant signal at the 5½ mile post indicated the close proximity of the home signal at the

This picture looking towards Bearley c.1952-53 shows the line climbing up to Captain's Hill with the three-arch road overbridge near Kinwarton on the skyline. The MR down distant signal was for the junction at Alcester. P. J. GARLAND

Taken from the same spot as the previous view but facing Alcester, this picture shows the farm track underbridge followed by the River Arrow bridge c.1952-53.
P. J. GARLAND

The River Arrow bridge on 5th July 1958. The repaired wing wall referred to in the text can clearly be seen on the left. This structure remains to this day carrying a footpath access across the river.
ROGER SELLICK

junction and this was followed by the River Arrow bridge at 5 miles 56¾ chains. This and the three-arch overbridge near Kinwarton were the largest bridge structures on the branch. The Arrow bridge consisted of a lattice girder span of 69ft 6in with red and blue brick abutments.

Former ganger Edward Booker recalled an incident during the 1930s, when one of the wing walls collapsed, and emergency repairs had been carried out by his gang after they had constructed a makeshift dam:

> 'The driver of the 7.35 p.m. down train from Bearley reported that the wing wall had fallen into the river. With the help of a bridge gang from Wolverhampton, we removed the track from the bridge and placed in position two timber baulks measuring 70ft long by 7in by 7in. We replaced the track, drove steel interlocking piles deep into the river bed around the fallen wing wall and filled the back with vast quantities of boulders and about a yard of cement to make a good job done!'

After crossing the River Arrow, the line began a sharp left-hand turn that took it through a full 90 degrees towards Alcester Junction; at this point down trains passed beneath a red-brick arched bridge that carried the A435 Alcester to Birmingham main road (formerly Icknield Street) across the branch on a skewed alignment.

This bridge, seen in 1952-53, carried the A435 Alcester–Birmingham road over the line. P. J. GARLAND

This view from the Alcester–Birmingham road bridge shows the branch curving to join the ex-MR Redditch–Evesham line. Note the PW trolley shed and sleeper decking in the centre of the picture and the siding connection to the GWR loco shed which is just visible on the left. This picture was taken in 1949. J. H. MOSS

THE ALCESTER BRANCH

Beyond the bridge, the line continued its southwards curve, and having passed a small wooden permanent way shed on the right-hand side, trains slowed as they approached the junction with the Midland Railway Ashchurch to Redditch line. Passing the Great Western locomotive shed on the left-hand side, down branch workings reached the MR at Alcester Junction.

Now running on Midland Railway (later LMS) metals, trains ran past the MR goods yard on the left-hand side and entered Alcester station. Here, some 6 miles 71 chains from Bearley, journeys over the Alcester branch came to an end.

This 1952-53 view was taken from near the loco shed looking towards Bearley with the Alcester–Birmingham bridge in the distance. The scotch block across the running line, adjacent to the MR home signal, marked the limit of Western Region and former GWR maintenance.
P. J. GARLAND

A 1952-53 photo of Alcester's MR-pattern branch down home signal. Note the lineside telephone box and the wire insulators and bars attached to the signal post.
P. J. GARLAND

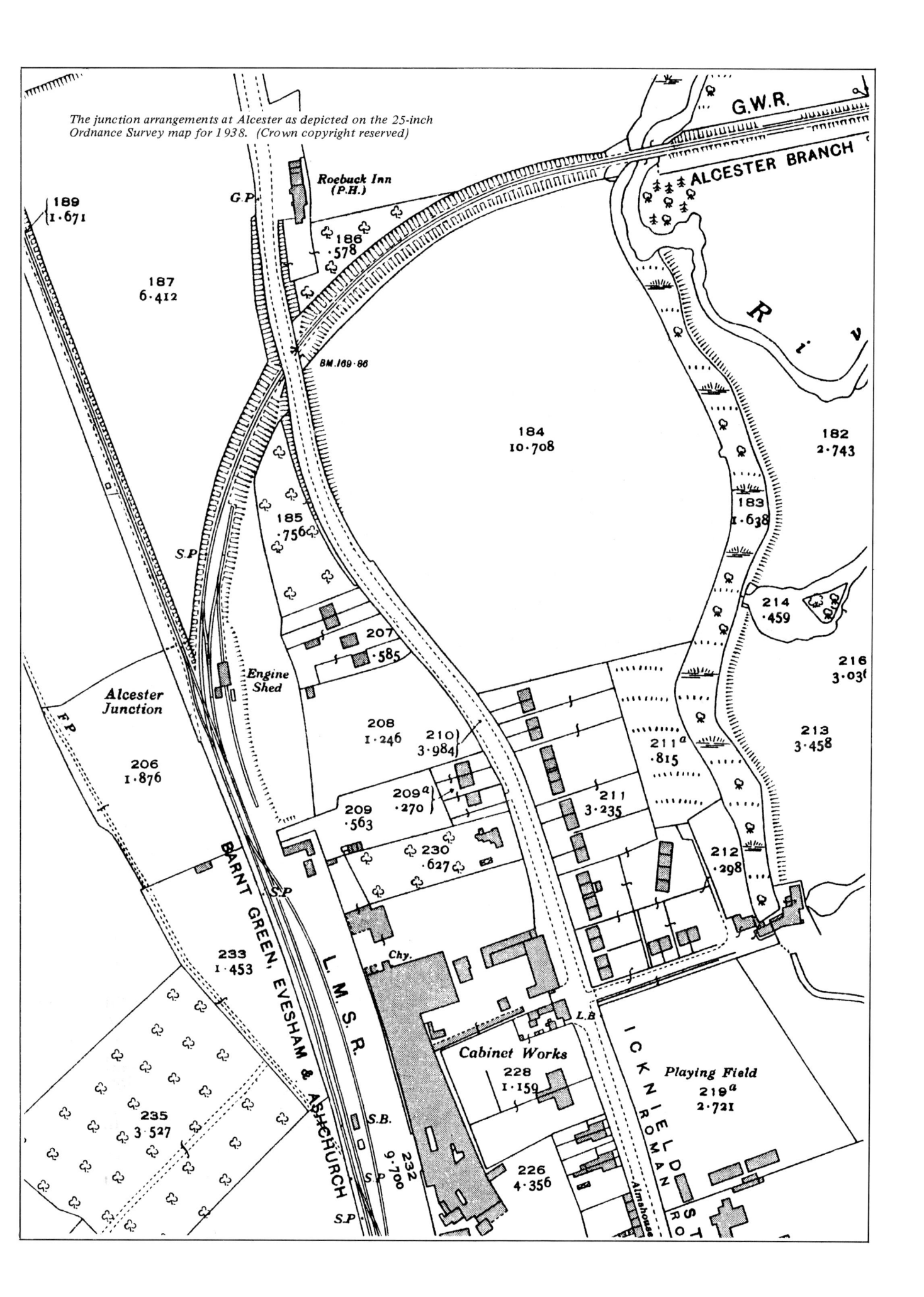

The junction arrangements at Alcester as depicted on the 25-inch Ordnance Survey map for 1938. (Crown copyright reserved)

The branch junction at Alcester, with the loco shed, water tank, pump house and the coal stage on 28th February 1953. The former junction signal box was situated just beyond the MR 64 milepost.
L&GRP

The GWR loco shed in August 1936. This brick-built structure measured approximately 38ft by 16ft at ground level, and it contained a 36ft inspection pit.
W. A. CAMWELL

ALCESTER STATION

Alcester station was built by the Evesham & Redditch Railway and opened for goods traffic on 16th June 1866, and for passengers on 17th September 1866; the line was worked by the Midland Railway from its inception. It was provided with a lengthy crossing loop, up and down platforms, extensive brick-built station buildings on the southbound side and a small waiting shelter on the northbound side. Connection between the up and down platforms was via a timbered barrow crossing at the south end of the station. The goods yard was provided with a brick-built goods shed, loading dock and cattle pens, whilst further along on the same side of the line was the GWR engine shed.

There was no separate platform for GWR branch trains, so after passengers and parcels had been unloaded in the

This was the view from the LMS 1932-built signal box window, taken on a warm summer's day in 1949, looking towards the junction, with the ex-MR line to Redditch stretching into the distance. The coal stacking ground on the extreme right was held by Shrimptons, whilst the hut and area beyond and underneath the trees was occupied by Butlers. Before the 1930s the area beyond the coal merchants huts was set aside for three oil storage tanks and auxiliary outbuildings. J. H. MOSS

This photograph, taken from a Birmingham-bound train during the 1950s, shows a single-line staff exchange taking place adjacent to the 1932 replacement signal box (opened on 24th April 1932). It also shows the signalman's coal and ash bunker and the corrugated-iron-built lamp hut.
COLLECTION R. J. ESSERY

main platforms, incoming GWR branch trains would either set back into the nearby goods yard to carry out any shunting that might be necessary or retire to the confines of the Great Western branch before working the next return trip on their own line.

For many years the station was signalled from two standard Midland Railway hip-roofed signal cabins, which presumably dated from the period 1884–1893 when the MR carried out a major resignalling programme. The single line was controlled by Midland-pattern tablet instruments, while the signals were typical MR lower quadrant semaphores.

In the early 1930s the LMS introduced several modifications to the signalling system on the Ashchurch to Redditch line and, although most of the Midland Railway signals at Alcester remained in operation, the two MR signal boxes were abolished, and in their place a single box was erected at the north end of the station on the down side in 1932. The new cabin was a gabled box, and its external appearance reflected London & North Western Railway practice (such LNWR-style boxes having been adopted by the LMS as a standard design in place of the earlier Midland Railway hip-roofed designs).

In architectural terms, the station building was clearly very different when compared to those at Bearley and Great Alne. It was an L-shaped structure incorporating a two-storey station master's house at the south end and a long, single-storey booking office portion to the north. The southern part dated from the opening of the Evesham & Redditch Railway in 1866, whereas the northern section incorporated the additional offices that had been required in connection with the opening of the Alcester Railway in 1876.

Although Alcester was never a 'joint' station in the fullest sense of the term, it was staffed by both Midland and Great Western employees. There were separate booking arrangements for the GWR line, and Great Western tickets were issued for journeys to Bearley and beyond via the Great Western route.

The Great Western provided its own station master who, in the 1920s, was Mr W. Everitt. In 1927 he moved to a new post at Bletchington (on the Oxford to Birmingham main line) and Mr J. N. Billington then came to Alcester from Bordesley Junction. These arrangements were brought to an end in April 1932 when the station was placed under LMS control, but records show that the GWR continued to employ a staff of two at the station until the closure of the branch in September 1939.

In the early years there were two Great Western train crews at Alcester in addition to the three men who worked at the nearby passenger station. The total GWR staffing establishment at Alcester around 1913 was thus a station master, one porter-guard, two drivers, two firemen and one guard. In 1911 the drivers were Mr G. Whitaker and Mr C. Stairmead. Later, around 1920, the regular driver was Charlie Harper, while the fireman and porter-guard were Mr Edmunds and Mr Hughes respectively.

THE LINE DESCRIBED

Another view from the signal box on the same summer's day, this time looking towards the station. The structure in the left background was occupied by Messrs. Rowley, the local abattoir. Note the MR-pattern gas lamp and signal and the thick privet hedge adjoining the 'boundary fence'.
J. H. MOSS

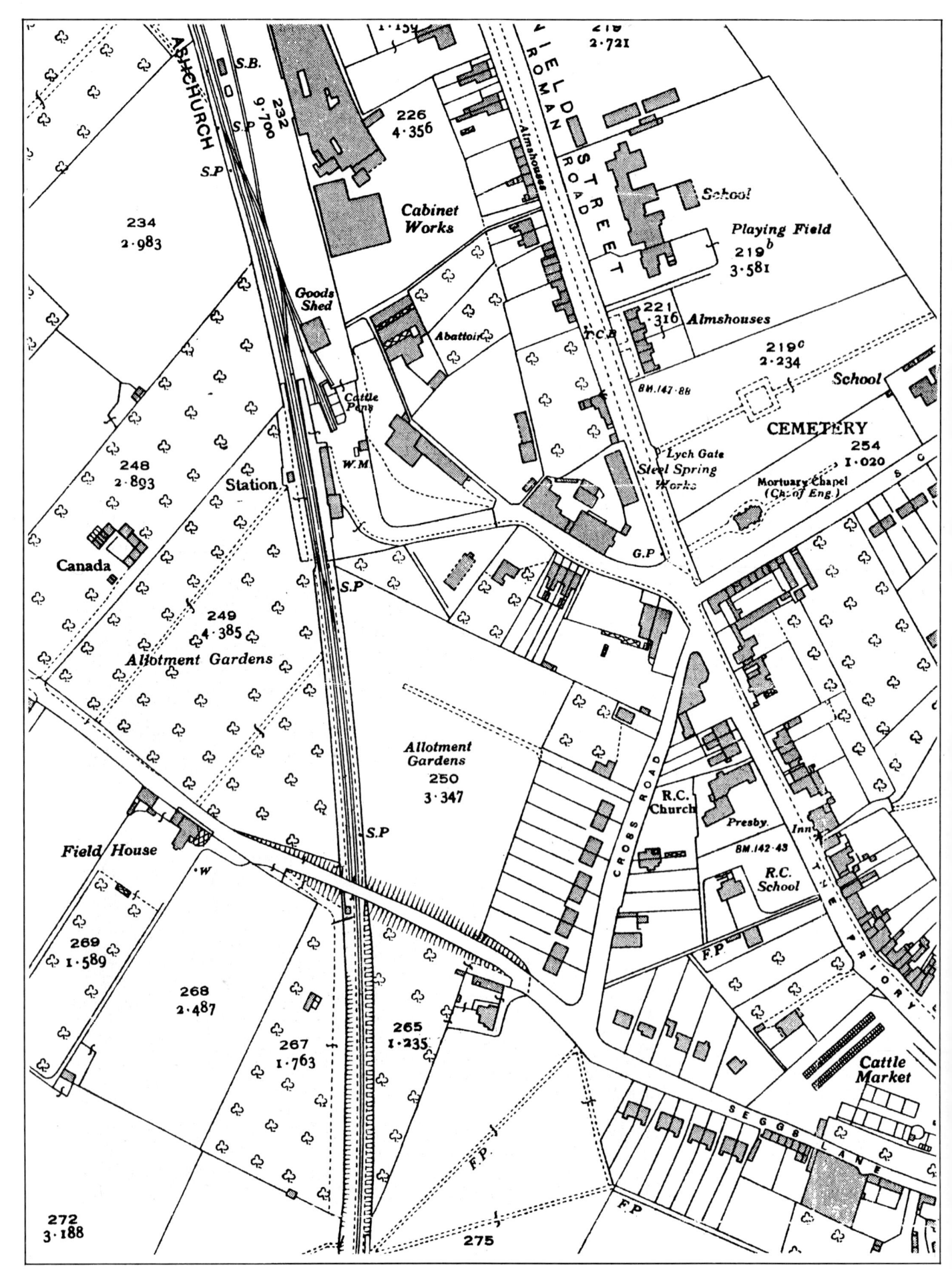

Taken from the 25-inch Ordnance Survey for 1938. (Crown copyright reserved)

William Hunt, who remembered the Alcester branch in the late 1920s and early 1930s, recalled that Mr Hughes had perfected the art of swinging aboard the train after it had started to move off from the platforms, which seemed, in the eyes of a child, 'a very fine and daring thing to do'!

'Mr Hughes was a splendid figure in his guard's uniform, complete with peaked cap, metal-buttoned coat, watch-chain, railway watch and whistle. He was always referred to by my mother as 'Mr Hughes, the Porter-Guard', presumably to distinguish him from other Hugheses in the town, and I always thought this title conferred upon him a status far above that of a mere guard, whereas I now suppose the reverse to be the case.'

The types of traffic handled included coal, timber and general merchandise. There was also a considerable amount of livestock traffic in connection with the local Co-operative Society, which received cattle for slaughter in its abattoir.

Alcester station, seen from the down platform, looking towards Evesham in 1949. J. H. MOSS

The station buildings and goods shed at Alcester were constructed in red brick with patterned slate roofs. This view of the up side waiting room was taken in 1962. J. H. MOSS

The forecourt elevation of the station buildings seen from the station approach on 19th April 1959. Alcester itself was situated to the east of the railway, and visitors arriving at the station by train did not have far to walk in order to reach the town centre. As mentioned in Chapter 1, Alcester was a small Warwickshire market town with a history dating back to Roman times. The town was remarkable chiefly for its timber-framed buildings, most of which dated back to the Tudor and Stuart periods. The Old Malt House, for example, could trace its history back to about 1500, whilst the Town Hall was a 17th-century building.

H. C. CASSERLEY

THE LINE DESCRIBED

A view from the end of the down platform, looking towards Evesham in the 1950s and featuring the standard Midland-pattern lower quadrant starting signal, complete with its distinctive spiked finial.

The situation regarding traffic statistics at Alcester is complicated by reason of the station's shared operation. The Great Western nevertheless managed to identify that proportion of passenger and freight traffic attributable to its own system, and in this respect Alcester was regarded as a conventional branch line terminus for accounting purposes, whatever traffic passed onto the GWR being counted separately.

In general, Alcester issued about 6,000 GWR tickets during the early 1930s, falling slightly to about 5,000 per annum during the later part of that decade. In 1932, for instance 6,321 ordinary tickets were issued, plus 47 season tickets, while in 1938 the corresponding figures were 5,221 tickets and 6 seasons.

Goods traffic attributable to the GWR line fluctuated throughout the years, a little over 5,000 tons of freight per annum being handled between 1930 and 1932, though only 2,049 tons was dealt with in 1936.

These figures suggest that Alcester was more important to the GWR as a source of passenger traffic than it was in relation to goods traffic. In this context it should be remembered that people wishing to travel to and from Stratford-on-Avon were offered a better service via the Great Western route than they were on the LMS lines via Broom Junction. Similarly, the GWR branch provided a useful link to Warwick and Leamington Spa for people wishing to visit these places for shopping or leisure purposes. On the other hand, the LMS system was useful for journeys to Redditch (where many Alcester residents worked), Evesham, Cheltenham or Gloucester, and in practice the bulk of Alcester's daily passenger business catered for regular travellers to these LMS destinations.

The Midland Railway bi-directional signal situated at the south end of the station bore the down advance starter and the up inner home. The red-brick bridge No. 42 carried a minor road from Alcester to Cold Comfort Farm. This picture was taken in 1958.
D. IBBOTSON

Churchward 2–6–2T No. 3152 hurrying past Bearley junctions with a Stratford–Birmingham semi-fast on 5th August 1946. The train comprised a four-coach set of Churchward suburban stock and a Collett four-coach suburban set at the rear, all in the wartime brown livery.
C. H. OLDHAM, CTY. MILLBROOK HOUSE

CHAPTER SIX
THE POSTWAR YEARS

The decaying remains of Aston Cantlow Halt as seen in April 1957, with the running line temporarily clear of wagons. The corrugated-iron waiting shelter and lamp hut were removed during the war years, probably about 1942-43. The halt was briefly reopened between October 1941 and 25th September 1942 in connection with the auto-worked GW workmen's trains from Leamington General to Great Alne for Maudslay factory workers.
JOHN EDGINGTON

The long procession of crippled wagons awaiting repair or scrapping was a familiar sight along the branch during the 1950s. This view was taken from the road overbridge adjacent to the remains of Aston Cantlow Halt.

THE end of the war in Europe in May 1945 was followed by the election of a new and radical Labour Government, that had promised to nationalise the railway system and other 'commanding heights of the economy'. This pledge was quickly put into effect, and on 1st January 1948 the Big Four railway companies were replaced by a state-run organisation known as British Railways. In reality this change of ownership did not give rise to any immediate changes, and the former Great Western Railway was painlessly transformed into the Western Region of British Railways.

The regular twice-weekly freight service to Great Alne had ceased by 1947, and by 1949 BR was working the residual goods line by 'special arrangement' in connection mainly with the carriage of sugar beet during the season from about four local farms, notably the Fennimores and Water Summers (from Haselor) conveyed in iron-wheel cart and horse. In September 1950 the Western Region Branch Line Committee therefore proposed that the entire line should be closed, leaving a truncated 400 yard length at the Alcester end for wagon storage.

Interestingly, BR seemed unwilling to close the branch in its entirety without first ensuring that there would no need for the line in the foreseeable future, and in this context Maudslay Motors Ltd were approached to see if they would consider making renewed use of rail transport for their factory at Great Alne; sadly, Maudslays intimated that they envisaged little further use for the railway, as all of their transport needs were being satisfied by road vehicles.

Having explored various options whereby the line might have been retained, BR announced that the branch would be closed to all traffic with effect from 1st March 1951, about two miles of line being retained at the eastern end for wagon storage as far as the Aston Cantlow river bridge, together with a similar length of line at the western end between Alcester Junction and a point on the western side of Great Alne level crossing. The intervening portion between Great Alne and the River Alne bridge at Aston Cantlow was abandoned, and subsequently lifted.

The eastern section of line between Bearley North Junction and Aston Cantlow continued to see sporadic movements of crippled or condemned wagons or vans, the

The Bearley North Curve looking towards the North Junction during the 1950s. The open wagons were stored in the mileage siding adjoining Bearley goods yard whilst the coaching stock in the distance was stored on the North Curve itself.　　BETTY CASTLE

The North Curve saw little use after the last war, apart from spells of wagon storage and occasional use for diversions and the stabling of the royal train. During two successive Sundays in May 1929, the curve was used for the last time for diversional purposes. This view, taken on 24th May, shows 'Castle' class No. 5079 Lysander cautiously negotiating the weed-stricken track of the North Curve with the 3.20 p.m. Wolverhampton to Paddington, looked on by other railway enthusiasts with cameras to record the scene.　　T. E. WILLIAMS/NRM

usual practice being for the 'cripples' to be propelled from Bearley North Junction towards the end of the line.

It is interesting to note that, although the Alcester branch was, strictly speaking, an 'uncoloured' route under the GWR system of route restrictions, the locomotives used during the 1950s were often '57XX' class 0–6–0PTs, which, as 'yellow' engines, would have been regarded as too heavy for the line when it was open for passenger traffic.

The branch was also used as an overnight stabling point between the Edstone Aqueduct and Aston Cantlow Halt for a royal train working on Wednesday 10th March 1954, on the occasion of a royal visit to the Midlands by HRH Princess Margaret.

CLOSURE AND AFTER

By the end of the 1960s the numbers of short-wheelbase loose-coupled goods wagons was being drastically reduced, with a corresponding reduction in the need for wagon storage sidings. The remaining sections of the branch were, moreover, allowed to deteriorate to such an extent that track renewal became uneconomic. The line was, in every sense of the term, redundant by 1960, and in that year BR decided that the fragmented branch would be closed in its entirety. It was officially taken out of use in August 1960 and track lifting was put into effect shortly afterwards. The connections at Bearley North Junction were removed on 28th August 1960, and Bearley North Junction Signal Box was closed in the following January.

THE BEARLEY NORTH CURVE

A similar fate befell the easternmost section of the former Alcester line, the curve between Bearley East and Bearley North junctions. Advertised passenger workings had ceased using this connection from 3rd May 1943, the last scheduled service being the 6.54 p.m. Henley-in-Arden to Bearley working, which returned as an empty stock working from Bearley to Earleswood Lakes, where it was stabled overnight. Thereafter, as we have seen, the curve had still been used by the Maudslay workmen's trains, and the freight service to Great Alne.

Following the official closure of the Alcester branch in March 1951 the curve was used to store crippled and surplus wagons, though it was specially cleared on several occasions during the 1950s for the overnight stabling of royal trains when members of the royal family visited Stratford-upon-Avon. It was also used by diverted main-line trains on two successive Sundays on 24th and 31st May 1959, when the Oxford to Birmingham route was closed due to engineering work at Rowington water troughs, and through services were routed over the North Warwickshire line and thence to Hatton via Bearley North and East junctions.

The very last passenger working to traverse the entire curve was a Stephenson Locomotive Society special that ran from Birmingham to Henley-in-Arden old station, and returned to Birmingham via the curve on Saturday 1st July 1959.

View from the parapet of the three-arch occupation bridge near Kinwarton, facing Alcester, showing the demolition contractors train in the distance during 1960. RICHARD KING
CTY. WARWICKSHIRE COUNTY RECORD OFFICE (PH417-30)

The last royal train to be stabled on the curve spent the night at Bearley on 22nd and 23rd October 1959 when HRH the Duke of Edinburgh visited the National Vegetable Research Station at Wellesbourne, the royal special being worked in and out via Bearley East Junction. The connections at each end of the curve were taken out of use in 1960 (at the same time as the Alcester branch connection), and the curve itself was removed shortly afterwards, thereby bringing to an end the life and history of the Alcester Railway

THE CONNECTING LINES

These closures and retractions left just six chains or so of the Alcester Railway in existence, the section concerned being the fragment that had been utilised during the construction of the North Warwickshire line at Bearley North Junction. Even this remaining fragment was threatened with closure during the anti-railway purges of the 1960s, when the government of the day was making no secret of its dislike of the nationalised railway system. The connecting lines at both ends of the Alcester route were threatened at this time. In the west, the passenger service between Redditch and Evesham was 'temporarily' withdrawn with effect from 1st October 1962, and 'official' closure was put into effect from 17th June 1963, when a replacement 'bus service was withdrawn; freight trains ran from Redditch to Alcester until 6th July 1964, after which Alcester station was closed in its entirety.

This photo was purchased as a postcard from Great Alne Post Office after conversion c.1956. COLLECTION GARTH TILT

In the east, the North Warwickshire line was repeatedly threatened with closure, though the former Stratford-upon-Avon Railway between Hatton and Stratford appeared to have a relatively safe future as the one remaining rail link to the popular tourist centre of Stratford-upon-Avon.

Bearley station was down-graded during the 1960s, when its goods yard was closed, though the station remained open as an unstaffed halt. Its platforms were shortened in December 1966, and in January 1969 the line was singled between Hatton and Bearley East Junction. This station is now merely a shadow of its former self. In May 1993 Bearley was served by seven up and six down services on Mondays to Saturdays, all of these being by request only; there was no Sunday service.

REMAINS

The abandoned line between Bearley and Alcester has slowly reverted to nature in the years that have elapsed since its final demise. The site of the junction between the GWR and Midland lines at Alcester was incorporated into a housing estate in the 1970s whilst, further east, modern factory developments have obliterated parts of the former route in the vicinity of the Arden Park Industrial Estate.

The 1 in 66 climb up through the cutting to Captain's Hill was filled in several years ago, and elsewhere the earthworks have been removed by farmers in search of ever-greater levels of profit from their highly-subsidised activities. At Aston Cantlow, the remains of the river bridge can still be seen, and at Great Alne the station building has been adapted for use as a private dwelling.

The former station was, for many years, the home of former BR fireman Walter Dawe, who had worked on the branch during its last days when it was reduced to siding status; the building was little-altered at the time of its initial conversion, and at the present time this original station building is perhaps the most interesting relic of the erstwhile Alcester Railway.

Ironically, the Edstone Aqueduct still towers above the North Warwickshire line at the site of Bearley North Junction, this supposedly 'obsolete' relic of the pre-railway age having survived long years of closure and abandonment until its restoration as part of the revived Stratford-upon-Avon Canal. The canal is today part of a busy network of waterways, and as such its future is assured; it saw the railway come and go, yet the waterway is itself a monument to the Industrial Age that brought both canals and railways into being to serve the transport needs of the world's first industrialised nation. To that extent, the great aqueduct – with a still extant fragment of the Alcester Railway only yards away – is today the most obvious and lasting relic of those far-off, Victorian days when the 'Alcester Coffee Pot' was an integral part of local life in this part of Warwickshire.

APPENDIX
SIGNALLING THE ALCESTER BRANCH
by GARTH H. TILT

From the opening in 1876, the single-line branch from Bearley to Alcester was worked as 'one engine in steam' with a wooden train staff. Bearley station was a crossing loop on the Hatton to Honeybourne branch and was worked by train staff and ticket between Hatton and Bearley with triangular staff and tickets coloured blue. The section Bearley to Stratford was also train staff and ticket with round staff and tickets coloured red. As there was no block telegraph, trains were worked by the 'time interval system'. Certainly by the 1880s there was a signal box at Great Alne to protect the level crossing, but it was neither a block nor staff post.

Following the 1889 Act the whole of the Hatton to Honeybourne section was converted to the electric train staff system in 1893. The sections between Hatton and Stratford were Hatton North-Claverdon, Claverdon-Bearley, Bearley-Wilmcote and Wilmcote-Stratford Goods Junction. Both Claverdon and Wilmcote boxes could switch out, long section staffs were provided between Hatton North and Bearley, and Bearley and Stratford Goods Junction. As neither Claverdon nor Wilmcote boxes were passing places, the extravagance of the long and short section working was soon dispensed with and both boxes were demoted to ground frames unlocked by keys on their respective staffs. In 1897 the staff section to Hatton was shortened to a new signal box at Hatton Branch Junction which opened with the new Hatton North Curve, the section into Hatton station now being double line. A ground frame existed between Claverdon and Bearley at Edstone Crossing working Up and Down distant signals. So as the century ended the GWR were already planning new lines to the West of England and South Wales from the Midlands. A completely new line from Honeybourne to Cheltenham and one from Tyseley to Bearley via Earlswood Lakes and Henley in Arden, with a triangular junction provided at Bearley, was envisaged. Also in connection with the new lines, the line from Bearley to Honeybourne was to be widened and doubled. The Alcester branch was to be improved and, in anticipation of the introduction of Electric Tablet Working, an experimental ground frame with tablet locking, the first on the GWR, was ordered for the existing siding at Great Alne in the winter of 1902/03. No doubt the tablet as opposed to the staff was preferred by the Midland Railway at Alcester. By December 1905 Tyers No. 6 tablet instruments were installed between Bearley Station and Alcester Junction signal boxes coupled with the Occupation Key system, with six intermediate key boxes. Midland Railway Tablet regulations were in force. The 'one engine in steam' wooden train staff, which by this time was square, painted red, was withdrawn.

Interior of Bearley West Junction signal box c.1930.
KIDDERMINSTER RAILWAY MUSEUM

In January 1907, to facilitate the construction of the new North Warwickshire line near the site of the later Bearley North Junction, a temporary contractors crossing with signal box containing 7 levers was brought into use. The trap points in the contractors line were locked by a tablet being out, and released by all tablets being in, plus the withdrawal of an occupation key which released a key lever in the locking frame. The box was not a staff or block post.

In association with these new works, the whole of the Honeybourne line south of Bearley was being widened to link up with the recently completed Cheltenham and Honeybourne line. On 17th May 1907 new junctions were cut in at the site of the new Bearley West Junction and in the following month the line was doubled from Bearley Station to Wilmcote. The former signal box at Wilmcote was reopened with an 11-lever frame and a new intermediate box at Bearley West Junction containing a 25-lever frame was opened. This worked a temporary single-line junction into the Alcester branch, which was slewed from the site of the future North Junction to enable the remainder of the branch into Bearley Station to be lowered and realigned into the new line under construction. The electric tablet working became Alcester Junction-Bearley West Junction, with the occupation key system retained. Alcester Branch trains were specially authorised to propel between Bearley West Jc and the Station box, which was now, renamed Bearley East Jc. All the new arrangements came into use on the 6th June 1907.

By November 1907 new junctions were cut in at the new Bearley North Jc and a new locking frame of 31 levers was installed in the East Junction box enabling the ground frame at the Hatton end of the station to be dispensed with. On 3rd November a new signal box containing 27 levers was partially brought into use at Wilmcote before the extension of the double line to Stratford Goods Jc a fortnight later on the 17th. A new down platform on the Stratford side of the overbridge had been brought into use there on 11th August; now a new up platform was brought into use opposite, enabling the old platform on the Bearley side of the bridge to be abandoned. Amongst all this feverish activity, part of the new North Warwickshire line was opened the following weekend on Sunday 24th November between Bearley North and West Junctions. At Bearley North Jc a new signal box containing 35 levers was opened, enabling the Alcester Branch trains to be returned to their direct route to Bearley East Jc. There were now two electric tablet sections, Alcester Jc-Bearley North and Bearley North-Bearley East. Double line block was in use to Bearley West. The temporary arrangements were now cancelled.

At Bearley North Jc (ordered as Alcester Jc incidentally) there were two double to single line junctions either side of the timber box which was on an embankment. Repeating junction home signals were installed, which was standard GWR practice on new work at the time. The Down Main Home signal was unusually high, with repeating junction homes with co-acting arms as the new line and the Alcester branch were crossed by the imposing aqueduct of the Stratford upon Avon canal.

The new North Warwickshire line was finally opened from Tyseley South to Bearley North on Sunday 8th December. Double-line block was brought into use from Bearley North to Henley in Arden and officially to

Bearley West on this date. Only ballast and materials trains were to use the line but under double-line disc block regulations. Later, through goods trains were allowed and in the spring of 1908 local goods trains were introduced. Finally, on 1st July 1908, through local and express passenger trains were inaugurated, the majority of the local trains running direct into Bearley station with the Alcester branch trains. Meantime, during April 1908, at Great Alne a second connection with ground frame was installed at the Bearley end of the yard.

Things soon settled down despite the new line being temporarily closed following serious landslips, particularly in the Shirley and Yardley Wood area. There was now a new double-track mainline from South Birmingham right through to Cheltenham Spa.

As the problems of the Great War increased, all services between Bearley North and Alcester Jc ceased on 1st January 1917 in a desperate attempt to provide extra track and materials for the War Effort. Only the junctions at each end were retained; the signalling on and off the branch at Bearley North were not removed until 12th February 1918. The curve to Bearley East had remained in use. To facilitate engine turning, as there was now no access onto the former branch, a crossover was laid on the Henley in Arden side of the box until hostilities ceased and the branch could be restored. This came about in 1922 when new signals were introduced at Bearley North including an additional Up Branch home signal with telephone provided on 14th December. The following day a 3-lever ground frame and crossing gates were installed at Spencer's Crossing working Up and Down distant signals and a gate bolt. A crossing indicator was provided. At Great Alne, two ground frames, East and West, provided to work the connections to the sidings. Finally, a Down distant signal, temporarily fixed at danger, was installed to protect Great Alne station. During the afternoon, a special train, engine and brake coach ran from Stratford in connection with the new works. Electric train tablet working was provided from Bearley North to Great Alne station office, but no signal box was provided, as the arrangements were temporary pending completion of the line to Alcester. The Occupation key boxes and telephones were restored. Most of the new signals provided were mounted on prefabricated concrete posts.

This view, taken inside Bearley East signal box in 1938, shows the single-line block instruments for the Bearley West Junction to Hatton section and for Bearley North Junction.
A. T. LOCKE, CTY.
KIDDERMINSTER
RAILWAY MUSEUM

Passenger and Goods services were resumed on the following Monday, 18th December. The next year saw the remainder of the branch restored. On Tuesday 31st July, the Signal Engineer had an occupation to transfer the electric tablet instrument from Great Alne to Alcester Jc signal box and restoring the Occupation key boxes and telephones. Pilot Working was in operation until completion of the works which also involved installing a new 3-lever ground frame at Great Alne Crossing to bolt the gates and work the Up and Down distant signals. A crossing indicator was provided. The following day all services were extended to Alcester.

During March 1928, yellow arms and lights were installed in place of red ones on all the Distant signals on the North Warwickshire line and the Alcester branch. In 1932 the LMS brought a new signal box into use at Alcester, replacing the existing Jc and Station boxes. The Tablet instrument and Occupation keys were transferred to the new box, being brought into use on 24th April. Sometime during this period a Down Branch Advanced Starting signal was installed at Bearley North to enable engines to stand on the branch and take water.

Following the outbreak of war in 1939, all services were withdrawn again between Bearley North and Alcester on 24th September. A few North Warwick line services still used the curve to Bearley East, however. With the establishment of a Shadow factory near Great Alne for Maudsley Motors Ltd, an unadvertised Workmen's Auto Passenger service was introduced from Leamington Spa to Great Alne in connection with an LMSR service from Coventry in May 1941, calling at Warwick and Aston Cantlow Halt. Subsequently public goods services were restored to Great Alne in September 1942, the morning Stratford-Leamington Goods running trips from Bearley as required. As there were no regular services beyond Great Alne and with due regard to wartime economy, the electric train tablet working was withdrawn and one 'engine in steam' working with a wooden train staff between Bearley North and Great Alne was introduced from Monday 18th May 1942. The Occupation key boxes were taken out of use and the tablet locks were replaced by staff locks on the ground frames at Great Alne. The section to Alcester remained closed but was retained for wagon storage. On 8th August 1943, at Bearley North a new ground disc, for backing movements from Down Main to Alcester branch, was brought into use to facilitate engines taking water and for essential refuging between trains. A similar disc had been installed earlier, for backing movements from Up Main to Bearley East to assist engine turning. Over the years more North Warwickshire passenger trains ran direct to and from Stratford as did some of the Alcester trips after 1922; the last to run into Bearley from the Henley in Arden direction ceased by 1943. During October 1944 the junctions at Bearley West were relaid and realigned with elbow points to improve speeds on the NW line. Earlier in the summer, the Great Alne Workmen's services were withdrawn from 1st July and never restored. The Goods services remained on an 'as required' basis until being officially withdrawn from 1st March 1951. The level crossing at Great Alne was subsequently removed and the road restored, the closed branch being retained as two separate sidings for storage purposes. For several years, the Aston Cantlow to Bearley North section was used for wagon storage and on at least one occasion on the night of 10/11th March 1954 the first 60 chains at the Bearley North end was used to accommodate the Royal Train.

The Bearley Curve had seen little use in postwar years apart from engine turning and the occasional goods trip to Great Alne. However, there was one final flurry of activity in 1959 after having been used for a number of years for storage purposes. For two Sundays in May, 24th and 31st, the Main Line north of Hatton was blocked to allow work on renewing Rowington water troughs, so all Paddington/Wolverhampton trains were diverted via Bearley East and North junctions and Henley in Arden to Tyseley. The last known passenger train on the curve ran on 1st July when the Stephenson Locomotive Society ran a special train in connection with the 50th anniversary of the opening of Moor Street station. Finally, the Royal Train stabled on the Curve on the night of 22nd/23rd October. It is thought that electric train token working had replaced the tablet working sometime after 1953. The trailing connection from the Up Main at Bearley North was taken out of use with the Alcester branch connections on 28th August 1960. The facing connection in the Down Main to the Curve were not taken out of use until 20th November. There was no reason to retain Bearley North box so it was taken out of use on 8th January 1961. The remains of the Curve disappeared in the early part of the decade as good services were withdrawn from Bearley on 20th May 1963. Further connections were removed and the East Junction box was abolished on 17th December 1967.

Wilmcote box had closed on 12th June 1966 and the block had been extended from Bearley West to Stratford East which had replaced Stratford Goods Junction in 1933. The branch to Hatton was doubled in 1939 having been worked by electric token since before 1921, and a new 37-lever frame was installed in Bearley East. An intermediate signal box was provided at Claverdon, and Hatton Branch box was renamed Hatton West. Claverdon box was closed 20th December 1953 and replaced by a ground frame released from Hatton West. Following withdrawal of goods facilities, Claverdon ground frame was abolished on 31st July 1964. The branch was again singled between Hatton West and Bearley West and worked by electric token from 12th January 1969, as part of the rationalisation work in connection with the forthcoming introduction of single-line track circuit block controlled from Saltley (Birmingham). This was brought into use on 1st September, Bearley West becoming the fringe box to Saltley. Although taken over from the WR by the LMR in 1963, only a few upper quadrant signals appeared. Western Region block regulations were retained until 1972.

The down distant for Spencer's Crossing. This was a standard GWR concrete-post signal dating from 1922.
P. J. GARLAND

Tailpiece:
To facilitate passenger train working at Bearley, regulation 5 'section clear but station or junction blocked' (the warning arrangement) was authorised in clear weather only between Bearley North and Henley in Arden on the Down Main for crossing Alcester branch trains, and between Bearley East and Claverdon, or boxes in rear, on the Down line, to save delays during shunting. Also between Bearley West and Henley in Arden when the North was switched out and to Claverdon or boxes in rear when the East was switched out for Down line trains. In the whole of the GWR Birmingham Division, regulation 5 was only authorised for passenger trains during fog and falling snow at four locations. One of these was from Bearley East to Bearley North for Alcester branch trains maintaining connections.

Bearley West box, which is still in use today, is the last link with the Alcester branch.

Acknowledgements
Many friends and colleagues have helped enormously over many years including; the late H.A.I. (Bert) Bromwich, W. Gillett, W.E. Holmes and J.P. Morris, the staff at BRB Records, Paddington, The Public Record Office, Ashridge and Kew, the former LMR Divisional S&T and Civil Engineers Depts. and the Chief Movements Office, Birmingham, whose generous time and facilities were much appreciated, M. Christensen, R.A. Cooke, M.R.L. Instone and C.E. Turner of the Signalling Record Society, D. Postle of the Kidderminster Railway Museum, J. Copsey, P. Jaques, D.E. Johnson and B.P. Stead. I have also consulted GWR, BRWR & LMR Public and Working Timetables, Appendices, Special Instructions, Notices, Plans, Correspondence Files and Reports.

Swindon documents officially record the internal dimensions of the brick-built Alcester engine shed as 38ft long, 16ft wide with heights to the top of the wall plate and ridge as 16ft and 22ft 6in respectively. The length of the track inside was 38ft and it incorporated a 36ft long inspection pit. There was also a 26ft long pit outside the shed for disposal. The base of the adjacent water tower used as a 'pumping engine house and stores' had internal dimensions of 12ft x 8ft with a height of 16ft to the bottom of the tank. A 20ft x 9ft brick-built coal stage with a wooden platform is recorded as being built in April 1900.

THE 'ECONOMIC' SYSTEM OF LINE MAINTENANCE

In an attempt to work the branch as cheaply as possible, in 1905 the line was equipped with Occupation Key boxes at regular intervals, and this enabled the route to be worked on the so-called 'Economic System' of line maintenance. Under this system, one gang of permanent way men could look after the entire branch, without the need to walk the entire line every day; instead, the ganger was provided with a four-wheel pumped trolley or 'pumper', which enabled the gang to reach any point on the branch by their own propulsive efforts. The pump trolley in question was officially known as a 'BUDA Inspection Car'.

To facilitate this method of operation the ganger had to be given possession of the single line, and this was achieved as simply and safely as possible by the use of the Occupation Key instruments, which were linked to the Electric Train Tablet system. When the trolley was taken out of its shed the key was withdrawn, which gave the permanent way gang possession of the line to travel to the point at which their work would be taking place. The trolley was then lifted off the track at the nearest available Occupation Key box, where the ganger surrendered the key and informed the signalman, by means of the telephone provided, that the line was now clear.

Removal of the Occupation Key effectively closed the single-line section between Bearley North and Alcester junctions, and no other train could use the line until the key was replaced into the system. Only then could the Electric Train Tablet be unlocked, and by this means the safe operation of the single line during engineering work was assured.

To enable the system to work, it was necessary for a sufficient number of Occupation Key boxes to be available, so that the ganger did not have to walk too far from the point at which track repairs were being carried out. Occupation Key huts were therefore installed at various places on the branch, including Bearley North Junction, Great Alne station and Alcester Junction. In addition, there were two huts between Bearley Junction and Great Alne, and another two between Great Alne and Alcester Junction.

Daily inspections of the entire branch were carried out by the ganger with the aid of a three-wheel rail-mounted inspection trolley. The heavier four-wheeled pump trolley was propelled by a cog system meshing with a crank, the latter being turned by up to six men pumping the handles provided.

Sources and Further Reading
The two main references to the Alcester branch in published works were an illustrated article by A. J. Fitzmaurice in the July 1956 *Model Railway News*, and an informative, two-part article entitled 'Railways in Shakespeare Country' in the July 1968 and August 1968 *Railway Magazine* by J. M. Tolson. Mr Tolson provided supplementary information in a letter published in the November 1968 edition of the same magazine. Other relevant articles include 'One Way for Henley', also by John Tolson, in the March 1985 *Railway Magazine*, and 'The Standard Buildings of William Clarke' in *British Railway Journal* No.8 (Summer 1985).

The primary sources for this present study included material in both public and private collections.

Material in the Public Records Office at Kew included the Alcester Railway Company minute books (PRO RAIL 6/1, RAIL 6/2 and RAIL 6/3) together with various files of correspondence from William Clarke and others (RAIL 6/14) and petitions, memorials and other items (RAIL 6/12, RAIL/13 and RAIL 6/6).

Other important sources of information in the PRO included the Great Western Railway traffic statistics (RAIL 266/46) and the 1925 Branch Line Report (RAIL 253/158).

These basic sources were supplemented by a variety of sources in private hands including maps, timetables, working notices, contemporary newspapers and journals, private notes, Acts of Parliament and photographs.

Thanks are due to a number of individuals who helped and assisted in different ways including John Copsey, Chris Turner, Richard Maund, John Tilsley, W. G. Hunt, D. G. Cox, Lens of Sutton, Edward Booker, Maurice Long, Mike Goddard, J. F. Burrell, John Platt, Walter Dawe, Pat Garland, Joe Moss, Reg Tedstone, Garth Tilt, Judy & Bob Smith and Kidderminster Railway Museum.

General background on Warwickshire was culled from numerous secondary sources including *Warwickshire* by J. Charles Cox, *Highways & Byways in Shakespeare's Country* by W. H. Hutton, *Leafy Warwickshire* by George Morley, *Warwickshire* by Arthur Mee, *Rambling in the Heart of England* by J. Nigel Hay and *Unknown Warwickshire* by M. Dormer Harris. The background to the bombing of Coventry in 1940 will be found in *Air Raid* by Norman Longmate (1976).

Finally, on a personal note, a certain amount of inspiration was also found in the earlier works of the Warwickshire novelist George Eliot (1819–1880), who drew heavily on her knowledge of local life for novels such as *The Mill on the Floss* and *Adam Bede*. Although the novelist was particularly associated with Coventry – which is probably the prototype for *Middlemarch* – one is also tempted to draw comparisons between Great Alne corn mill and the *Mill on the Floss*. (The social background and relationships between the millers in the novel and their 'socially superior' neighbours probably echoes the relationship between the Spencers and their fellow railway promoters during the 1870s!)

A Stratford–Alcester train at Bearley North Junction c.1937.

ALCESTER BRANCH—Single Line.

Service worked by an Auto Engine and Trailer, stabled at Alcester.

WEEK DAYS ONLY.

Mile post Mileage. M. C.		Ruling Gradient 1 in		B MXD A.M.	B Auto. A.M.	B Auto. P.M.	B MXD P.M. SX	B Auto. P.M. SO	B Auto. P.M.	B Auto. P.M. SX	B Auto. P.M. SO
—	Stratford o/A.	—	dep.	—	11 23	—	—	3 5	—	—	7 5
—	Wilmcote	—	,,	—	11 29	—	—	3 13	—	—	7 12
—	Bearley West	—	pass	—	11 33	—	—	3 16	—	—	7 15
—	Bearley	135F	dep.	9 36	11V36	1 22	3 5	—	4 45	7 32	7¶32
—	Bearley N. Jct.	75F	pass	C9 38S	C11 38S	C1 24S	C3 8S	C3 17S	C4 47S	C7 34S	C7 34S
1 38	Aston Cantlow	132F	dep.	9 47	11 43	1 32½	3 17	3 25½	4 52½	7 39½	7 39½
3 58	Great Alne	66F	dep.	9 58	11 51	1 40	3 28	3 33	5 0	7 50	7 50
6 0	Alcester	—	arr.	10 6	11 59	1 48	3 36	3 41	5 8	7 58	7 58

		Ruling Gradient 1 in		B Auto. A.M.	B Auto. A.M.	B Auto. P.M.	B MXD P.M. SX	B Auto. P.M. SO	B Auto. P.M. SO	B Auto. P.M.	B MXD P.M. SX
Alcester	....	66R	dep.	7 57	10 17	12 43	2 2	2 5	4Y2	5 40	5 40
Great Alne	..	132R	dep.	8 5½	10 25½	12 51½	2 13½	2 13½	4 10½	5 48½	6 0
Aston Cantlow	....	75R	dep.	8 13	10 33	12 59	2 21	2 21	4 18	5 56	6 8½
Bearley N. Jct.	..	135R	pass	C8 18S	C10 38S	C1 4S	C2 28S	C2 26S	C4 26S	C6 4S	C6 17S
Bearley	....	—	arr.	8 20	10Z40	1 6	2 30	—	4 28	—	6 20
Bearley West	..	—	pass	—	10 42½	—	—	2 27	—	6 5	—
Wilmcote	....	—	arr.	—	—	—	—	2 30	—	6 8	—
Stratford-on-Avon	..	—	arr.	—	10 50	—	—	2 35	—	6 13	—

¶ Bearley arrive 7.16 p.m.   V Via Bearley Station arrive 11.34 a.m.

Y Saturdays Alcester depart 3.55 p.m. as Mixed Train.   Z Depart 10.41 a.m.

Taken from Working Timetable for Winter 1938.